# E. E. CUMMINGS

## COLLECTED POEMS

### 1922–1938

# E. E. CUMMINGS

# COLLECTED POEMS
# 1922–1938

Book-of-the-Month Club    New York

# Contents

# Introduction

The poems to come are for you and for me and are not for mostpeople

—it's no use trying to pretend that mostpeople and ourselves are alike. Mostpeople have less in common with ourselves than the squarerootofminusone. You and I are human beings;mostpeople are snobs.

Take the matter of being born. What does being born mean to mostpeople? Catastrophe unmitigated. Socialrevolution. The cultured aristocrat yanked out of his hyperexclusively ultravoluptuous superpalazzo,and dumped into an incredibly vulgar detentioncamp swarming with every conceivable species of undesirable organism. Mostpeople fancy a guaranteed birthproof safetysuit of nondestructible selflessness. If mostpeople were to be born twice they'd improbably call it dying—

you and I are not snobs. We can never be born enough. We are human beings;for whom birth is a supremely welcome mystery,the mystery of growing:the mystery which happens only and whenever we are faithful to ourselves. You and I wear the dangerous looseness of doom and find it becoming. Life,for eternal us,is now;and now is much too busy being a little more than everything to seem anything,catastrophic included.

Life,for mostpeople,simply isn't. Take the socalled standardofliving. What do mostpeople mean by "living"? They don't mean living. They mean the latest and closest plural approximation to singular prenatal passivity which science,in its finite but unbounded wisdom,has succeeded in selling their wives. If science could fail,a mountain's a mammal. Mostpeople's wives can spot a genuine delusion of embryonic omnipotence immediately and will accept no substitutes

—luckily for us,a mountain is a mammal. The plusorminus movie to end moving,the strictly scientific parlourgame of real unreality,the tyranny conceived in misconception and dedicated to the proposition that every man is a woman and any woman a king,hasn't a wheel to stand on. What their most synthetic not to mention transparent majesty,mrsandmr collective foetus,would improbably call a ghost is walking. He isn't an undream of anaesthetized impersons,or a cosmic comfortstation,or a transcendentally sterilized lookiesoundiefeelietastiesmellie. He is a healthily complex,a naturally homogeneous, citizen of immortality. The now of his each pitying free imperfect gesture,his any birth or breathing,insults perfected inframortally millenniums of slavishness. He is a little more than everything,he is democracy;he is alive:he is ourselves.

Miracles are to come. With you I leave a remembrance of miracles:they are by somebody who can love and who shall be continually reborn,a human being;somebody who said to those near him,when his fingers would not hold a brush "tie it into my hand"—

nothing proving or sick or partial. Nothing false,nothing difficult or easy or small or colossal. Nothing ordinary or extraordinary,nothing emptied or filled,real or unreal; nothing feeble and known or clumsy and guessed. Everywhere tints childrening,innocent spontaneous,true. Nowhere possibly what flesh and impossibly such a garden, but actually flowers which breasts are among the very mouths of light. Nothing believed or doubted;brain over heart,surface:nowhere hating or to fear;shadow,mind without soul. Only how measureless cool flames of making;only each other building always distinct selves of mutual entirely opening;only alive. Never the murdered finalities of wherewhen and yesno,impotent nongames of wrongright and rightwrong;never to gain or pause,never the soft adventure of undoom,greedy anguishes and cringing ecstasies of inexistence;never to rest and never to have:only to grow.

Always the beautiful answer who asks a more beautiful question

E. E. CUMMINGS

# E. E. CUMMINGS

## COLLECTED POEMS

### 1922–1938

# Tulips
# and Chimneys

POEMS 1 TO 47

# 1

(thee will i praise between those rivers whose
white voices pass upon forgetting(fail
me not)whose courseless waters are a gloat
of silver;o'er whose night three willows wail,
a slender dimness in the unshapeful hour
making dear moan in tones of stroked flower;
let not thy lust one threaded moment lose:
haste)the very shadowy sheep float
free upon terrific pastures pale,

whose tall mysterious shepherd lifts a cheek
teartroubled to the momentary wind
with guiding smile,lips wisely minced for blown
kisses,condemnatory fingers thinned
of pity—so he stands counting the moved
myriads wonderfully loved,
(hasten,it is the moment which shall seek
all blossoms that do learn,scents of not known
musics in whose careful eyes are dinned;

and the people of perfect darkness fills
his mind who will their hungering whispers hear
with weepings soundless,saying of "alas
we were chaste on earth we ghosts:hark to the sheer
cadence of our gray flesh in the gloom!
and still to be immortal is our doom;
but a rain frailly raging whom the hills
sink into and their sunsets,it shall pass.
Our feet tread sleepless meadows sweet with fear")

then be with me:unseriously seem
by the perusing greenness of thy thought
my golden soul fabulously to glue
in a superior terror;be thy taut
flesh silver,like the currency of faint
cities eternal—ere the sinless taint
of thy long sinful arms about me dream
shall my love wholly taste thee as a new
wine from steep hills by darkness softly brought—

(be with me in the sacred witchery
of almostness which May makes follow soon
on the sweet heels of passed afterday,
clothe thy soul's coming merely,with a croon
of mingling robes musically revealed
in rareness:let thy twain eyes deeply wield
a noise of petals falling silently
through the far-spaced possible nearaway
from huge trees drenched by a rounding moon)

# 2

---

Thy fingers make early flowers of
all things.
thy hair mostly the hours love:
a smoothness which
sings,saying
(though love be a day)
do not fear,we will go amaying.

thy whitest feet crisply are straying.
Always
thy moist eyes are at kisses playing,
whose strangeness much
says;singing
(though love be a day)
for which girl art thou flowers bringing?

To be thy lips is a sweet thing
and small.
Death,Thee i call rich beyond wishing
if this thou catch,
else missing.
(though love be a day
and life be nothing,it shall not stop kissing).

# 3

---

Tumbling-hair
                picker of buttercups
                              violets
dandelions
And the big bullying daisies
                            through the field wonderful
with eyes a little sorry
Another comes
                also picking flowers

# 4

my love
thy hair is one kingdom
  the king whereof is darkness
thy forehead is a flight of flowers

thy head is a quick forest
  filled with sleeping birds
thy breasts are swarms of white bees
  upon the bough of thy body
thy body to me is April
in whose armpits is the approach of spring

thy thighs are white horses yoked to a chariot
  of kings
they are the striking of a good minstrel
between them is always a pleasant song

my love
thy head is a casket
  of the cool jewel of thy mind
the hair of thy head is one warrior
  innocent of defeat
thy hair upon thy shoulders is an army
  with victory and with trumpets

thy legs are the trees of dreaming
whose fruit is the very eatage of forgetfulness

thy lips are satraps in scarlet
  in whose kiss is the combining of kings
thy wrists
are holy
  which are the keepers of the keys of thy blood
thy feet upon thy ankles are flowers in vases
  of silver

in thy beauty is the dilemma of flutes

thy eyes are the betrayal
of bells comprehended through incense

# 5

it is at moments after i have dreamed
of the rare entertainment of your eyes,
when(being fool to fancy)i have deemed

with your peculiar mouth my heart my heart made wise;
at moments when the glassy darkness holds

the genuine apparition of your smile
(it was through tears always)and silence moulds
such strangeness as was mine a little while;

moments when my once more illustrious arms
are filled with fascination,when my breast
wears the intolerant brightness of your charms:

one pierced moment whiter than the rest

—turning from the tremendous lie of sleep
i watch the roses of the day grow deep.

# 6

---

All in green went my love riding
on a great horse of gold
into the silver dawn.

four lean hounds crouched low and smiling
the merry deer ran before.

Fleeter be they than dappled dreams
the swift sweet deer
the red rare deer.

Four red roebuck at a white water
the cruel bugle sang before.

Horn at hip went my love riding
riding the echo down
into the silver dawn.

four lean hounds crouched low and smiling
the level meadows ran before.

Softer be they than slippered sleep
the lean lithe deer
the fleet flown deer.

Four fleet does at a gold valley
the famished arrow sang before.

Bow at belt went my love riding
riding the mountain down
into the silver dawn.

four lean hounds crouched low and smiling
the sheer peaks ran before.

Paler be they than daunting death
the sleek slim deer
the tall tense deer.

Four tall stags at a green mountain
the lucky hunter sang before.

All in green went my love riding
on a great horse of gold
into the silver dawn.

four lean hounds crouched low and smiling
my heart fell dead before.

god gloats upon Her stunning flesh.   Upon
the reachings of Her green body among
unseen things,things obscene (Whose fingers young

the caving ages curiously con)

—but the lunge of Her hunger softly flung
over the gasping shores
                              leaves his smile wan,
and his blood stopped hears in the frail anon

the shovings and the lovings of Her tongue.

god Is The Sea.   All terrors of his being
quake before this its hideous Work most old
Whose battening gesture prophesies a freeing

of ghostly chaos
                       in this dangerous night
through moaned space god worships God—

                                              (behold!
where chaste stars writhe captured in brightening fright)

# 8

when citied day with the sonorous homes
of light swiftly sinks in the sorrowful hour,
thy counted petals O tremendous flower
on whose huge heart prospecting darkness roams

torture my spirit with the exquisite froms
and whithers of existence,
                     as by shores
soundless,the unspeaking watcher who adores

perceived sails whose mighty brightness dumbs

the utterance of his soul—so even i
wholly chained to a grave astonishment
feel in my being the delirious smart

of thrilled ecstasy,where sea and sky
marry—
               to know the white ship of thy heart

on frailer ports of costlier commerce bent

# 9

listen
beloved
i dreamed
   it appeared that you thought to
   escape me and became a great
   lily atilt on
   insolent
   waters      but i was aware of
   fragrance and i came riding upon
   a horse of porphyry      into the
   waters i rode down the red
   horse shrieking      from splintering
   foam caught you clutched you upon my
   mouth
listen
beloved
   i dreamed      in my dream you had
   desire to thwart me and became
   a little bird and hid
   in a tree of tall marble
   from a great way i distinguished
   singing and i came
   riding upon a scarlet sunset
   trampling the night      easily
   from the shocked impossible
   tower i caught
   you strained you
   broke you upon my blood
listen
   beloved i dreamed
   i thought you would have deceived
   me and became a star in the kingdom
   of heaven
   through day and space i saw you close
   your eyes      and i came riding

upon a thousand crimson years arched with agony
i reined them in tottering before
the throne and as
they shied at the automaton moon from
the transplendent hand of sombre god
i picked you
as an apple is picked by the little peasants for their girls

# 10

of evident invisibles
exquisite the hovering

at the dark portals

of hurt girl eyes


sincere with wonder

a poise a wounding
a beautiful suppression

the accurate boy mouth


now droops the faun head

now the intimate flower dreams

of parted lips
dim upon the syrinx

# 11

Doll's boy 's asleep
under a stile
he sees eight and twenty
ladies in a line

the first lady
says to nine ladies
his lips drink water
but his heart drinks wine

the tenth lady
says to nine ladies
they must chain his foot
for his wrist 's too fine

the nineteenth
says to nine ladies
you take his mouth
for his eyes are mine.

Doll's boy 's asleep
under the stile
for every mile the feet go
the heart goes nine

# 12

---

by little accurate saints thickly which tread
the serene nervous light of paradise—
by angelfaces clustered like bright lice

about god's capable dull important head—
by on whom glories whisperingly impinge
(god's pretty mother)but may not confuse

the clever hair nor rout the young mouth whose
lips begin a smile exactly strange—
this painter should have loved my lady.
And by this throat a little suddenly lifted

in singing—hands fragile whom almost tire
the sleepshaped lilies—

                  should my lady's body
with these frail ladies dangerously respire:

impeccable girls in raiment laughter-gifted.

# 13

the hours rise up putting off stars and it is
dawn
into the street of the sky light walks scattering poems

on earth a candle is
extinguished      the city
wakes
with a song upon her
mouth having death in her eyes

and it is dawn
the world
goes forth to murder dreams....

i see in the street where strong
men are digging bread
and i see the brutal faces of
people contented hideous hopeless cruel happy

and it is day,

in the mirror
i see a frail
man
dreaming
dreams
dreams in the mirror

and it
is dusk      on earth

a candle is lighted
and it is dark.
the people are in their houses
the frail man is in his bed
the city

sleeps with death upon her mouth having a song in her eyes
the hours descend,
putting on stàrs....

in the street of the sky night walks scattering poems

# 14

beyond the brittle towns asleep
i look where stealing needles of foam
in the last light

thread the creeping shores


as out of dumb strong hands infinite

the erect deep upon me
in the last light
pours its eyeless miles


the chattering sunset ludicrously
dies,i hear only tidewings

in the last light
twitching at the world

# 15

Always before your voice my soul
half-beautiful and wholly droll
is as some smooth and awkward foal,
whereof young moons begin
the newness of his skin,

so of my stupid sincere youth
the exquisite failure uncouth
discovers a trembling and smooth
Unstrength,against the strong
silences of your song;

or as a single lamb whose sheen
of full unsheared fleece is mean
beside its lovelier friends,between
your thoughts more white than wool
My thought is sorrowful:

but my heart smote in trembling thirds
of anguish quivers to your words,
As to a flight of thirty birds
shakes with a thickening fright
the sudden fooled light.

it is the autumn of a year:
When through the thin air stooped with fear,
across the harvest whitely peer
empty of surprise
death's faultless eyes

(whose hand my folded soul shall know
while on faint hills do frailly go
The peaceful terrors of the snow,
and before your dead face
which sleeps,a dream shall pass)

and these my days their sounds and flowers
Fall in a pride of petaled hours,
like flowers at the feet of mowers
whose bodies strong with love
through meadows hugely move.

yet what am i that such and such
mysteries very simply touch
me,whose heart-wholeness overmuch
Expects of your hair pale,
a terror musical?

while in an earthless hour my fond
soul seriously yearns beyond
this fern of sunset frond on frond
opening in a rare
Slowness of gloried air...

The flute of morning stilled in noon—
noon the implacable bassoon—
now Twilight seeks the thrill of moon,
washed with a wild and thin
despair of violin

# 16

---

when god lets my body be

From each brave eye shall sprout a tree
fruit that dangles therefrom

the purpled world will dance upon
Between my lips which did sing

a rose shall beget the spring
that maidens whom passion wastes

will lay between their little breasts
My strong fingers beneath the snow

Into strenuous birds shall go
my love walking in the grass

their wings will touch with her face
and all the while shall my heart be

With the bulge and nuzzle of the sea

# 17

a connotation of infinity
sharpens the temporal splendor of this night

when souls which have forgot frivolity
in lowliness,noting the fatal flight
of worlds whereto this earth's a hurled dream

down eager avenues of lifelessness

consider for how much themselves shall gleam,
in the poised radiance of perpetualness.
When what's in velvet beyond doomed thought

is like a woman amorous to be known;
and man,whose here is alway worse than naught,
feels the tremendous yonder for his own—

on such a night the sea through her blind miles

of crumbling silence seriously smiles

# 18

the moon is hiding in
her hair.
The
lily
of heaven
full of all dreams,
draws down.

cover her briefness in singing
close her with intricate faint birds
by daisies and twilights
Deepen her,

Recite
upon her
flesh
the rain's

pearls singly-whispering.

# 19

the glory is fallen out of
the sky the last immortal
leaf
is

dead and the gold
year
a formal spasm
in the

dust
this is the passing of all shining things
therefore we also
blandly

into receptive
earth,O let
us
descend

take
shimmering wind
these fragile splendors from
us crumple them hide

them in thy breath drive
them in nothingness
for we
would sleep

this is the passing of all shining things
no lingering no backward-
wondering be unto
us O

soul,but straight
glad feet fearruining
and glorygirded
faces

lead us
into the
serious
steep

darkness

a wind has blown the rain away and blown
the sky away and all the leaves away,
and the trees stand.   I think i too have known
autumn too long

                (and what have you to say,
wind wind wind—did you love somebody
and have you the petal of somewhere in your heart
pinched from dumb summer?
                        O crazy daddy
of death dance cruelly for us and start

the last leaf whirling in the final brain
of air!)Let us as we have seen see
doom's integration.........a wind has blown the rain

away and the leaves and the sky and the
trees stand:
                the trees stand.   The trees,
suddenly wait against the moon's face.

# 21

O sweet spontaneous
earth how often have
the
doting

      fingers of
prurient philosophers pinched
and
poked

thee
,has the naughty thumb
of science prodded
thy

     beauty    .how
often have religions taken
thee upon their scraggy knees
squeezing and

buffeting thee that thou mightest conceive
gods
    (but
true

to the incomparable
couch of death thy
rhythmic
lover

      thou answerest

them only with

          spring)

# 22

but the other
day i was passing a certain
gate,     rain
fell(as it will

in spring)
ropes
of silver gliding from sunny
thunder into freshness

as if god's flowers were
pulling upon bells of
gold     i looked
up

and
thought to myself     Death
and will You with
elaborate fingers possibly touch

the pink hollyhock existence whose
pansy eyes look from morning till
night into the street
unchangingly     the always

old lady always sitting in her
gentle window like
a reminiscence
partaken

softly     at whose gate smile
always the chosen
flowers of reminding

any man is wonderful
and a formula
a bit of tobacco and gladness
plus little derricks of gesture

any skyscraper
bulges in the looseness of morning
but in twilight becomes
unutterably crisp

a thing,
which tightens
caught
in the hoisting light

any woman is smooth and ridiculous
a polite uproar of knuckling silent planes
a nudging bulb silkenly brutal
a devout flexion

# 24

hist      whist
little ghostthings
tip-toe
twinkle-toe

little twitchy
witches and tingling
goblins
hob-a-nob      hob-a-nob

little hoppy happy
toad in tweeds
tweeds
little itchy mousies

with scuttling
eyes      rustle and run      and
hidehidehide
whisk

whisk      look out for the old woman
with the wart on her nose
what she'll do to yer
nobody knows

for she knows the devil      ooch
the devil      ouch
the devil
ach      the great

green
dancing
devil
devil

devil
devil


        wheeEEE

# 25

stinging
gold swarms
upon the spires
silver

     chants the litanies the
great bells are ringing with rose
the lewd fat bells
             and a tall

wind
is dragging
the
sea

with

dream

-S

spring omnipotent goddess thou dost
inveigle into crossing sidewalks the
unwary june-bug and the frivolous angleworm
thou dost persuade to serenade his
lady the musical tom-cat,thou stuffest
the parks with overgrown pimply
cavaliers and gumchewing giggly
girls and not content
Spring,with this
thou hangest canary-birds in parlor windows

spring slattern of seasons you
have dirty legs and a muddy
petticoat,drowsy is your
mouth your eyes are sticky
with dreams and you have
a sloppy body
from being brought to bed of crocuses
When you sing in your whiskey-voice

                                       the grass
rises on the head of the earth
and all the trees are put on edge

spring,
of the jostle of
thy breasts and the slobber
of your thighs
i am so very
                    glad that the soul inside me Hollers
for thou comest and your hands
are the snow
and thy fingers are the rain,
and i hear
the screech of dissonant
flowers,and most of all
i hear your stepping
                    freakish feet
                    feet incorrigible
ragging the world,

at the head of this street a gasping organ is waving moth-eaten tunes.  a fattish hand turns the crank;the box spouts fairies,out of it sour gnomes tumble clumsily,the little box is spilling rancid elves upon neat sunlight into the flower-stricken air which is filthy with agile swarming sonal creatures

—Children,stand with circular frightened faces glaring at the shabby tiny smiling,man in whose hand the crank goes desperately,round and round pointing to the queer monkey

(if you toss him a coin he will pick it cleverly from,the air and stuff it seriously in,his minute pocket)Sometimes he does not catch a piece of money and then his master will yell at him over the music and jerk the little string and the monkey will sit,up,and look at,you with his solemn blinky eyeswhichneversmile and after he has caught a,penny or three,pennies he will be thrown a peanut (which he will open skilfully with his,mouth carefully holding,it,in his little toylike hand)and then he will stiff-ly throw the shell away with a small bored gesture that makes the children laugh.

But i don't,the crank goes round desperate elves and hopeless gnomes and frantic fairies gush clumsily from the battered box fattish and mysterious the flowerstricken sunlight is thickening dizzily is reeling gently the street and the children and the monkeyandtheorgan and the man are dancing slowly are tottering up and down in a trembly mist of atrocious melody....tiniest dead tunes crawl upon my face my hair is lousy with mutilated singing microscopic things in my ears scramble faintly tickling putrescent atomies,

              and

                    i feel the jerk of the little string!

the tiny smiling shabby man is yelling over the music
i understand him i shove my round red hat back on
my head i sit up and blink at you with my solemn
eyeswhichneversmile

yes,By god.
for i am they are pointing at the queer monkey with a little
oldish doll-like face and hairy arms like an ogre and
rubbercoloured hands and feet filled with quick fingers
and a remarkable tail which is allbyitself alive.(and he has
a little red coat with i have a real pocket in it and the
round funny hat with a big feather is tied under myhis
chin.)     that climbs and cries and runs and floats like a
toy on the end of a string

the Cambridge ladies who live in furnished souls
are unbeautiful and have comfortable minds
(also,with the church's protestant blessings
daughters,unscented shapeless spirited)
they believe in Christ and Longfellow,both dead,
are invariably interested in so many things—
at the present writing one still finds
delighted fingers knitting for the is it Poles?
perhaps.   While permanent faces coyly bandy
scandal of Mrs. N and Professor D
....the Cambridge ladies do not care,above
Cambridge if sometimes in its box of
sky lavender and cornerless,the
moon rattles like a fragment of angry candy

i was considering how
within night's loose
sack a star's
nibbling in-

fin
-i-
tes-
i
-mal-
ly devours

darkness the
hungry star
which
will e

-ven
tu-
al
-ly jiggle
the bait of
dawn and be jerked

into

eternity. when over my head a
shooting
star
Bur     s

      (t
         into a stale shriek
like an alarm-clock)

# 30

in Just-
spring     when the world is mud-
luscious the little
lame balloonman

whistles     far     and wee

and eddieandbill come
running from marbles and
piracies and it's
spring

when the world is puddle-wonderful

the queer
old balloonman whistles
far     and     wee
and bettyandisbel come dancing

from hop-scotch and jump-rope and

it's
spring
and
    the

      goat-footed

balloonMan     whistles
far
and
wee

# 31

Buffalo Bill 's
defunct
         who used to
         ride a watersmooth-silver
                              stallion
and break onetwothreefourfive pigeonsjustlikethat
                                        Jesus

he was a handsome man
                     and what i want to know is
how do you like your blueeyed boy
Mister Death

# 32

ladies and gentlemen this little girl
with the good teeth and small important breasts
(is it the Frolic or the Century whirl?
one's memory indignantly protests)
this little dancer with the tightened eyes
crisp ogling shoulders and the ripe quite too
large lips always clenched faintly,wishes you
with all her fragile might to not surmise
she dreamed one afternoon

                      ....or maybe read?

of a time when the beautiful most of her
(this here and This,do you get me?)
will maybe dance and maybe sing and be
absitively posolutely dead,
like Coney Island in winter

into the strenuous briefness
Life:
handorgans and April
darkness,friends

i charge laughing.
Into the hair-thin tints
of yellow dawn,
into the women-coloured twilight

i smilingly
glide.   I
into the big vermilion departure
swim,sayingly;

(Do you think?)the
i do,world
is probably made
of roses & hello:

(of solongs and,ashes)

# 34

---

"kitty". sixteen,5'1",white,prostitute.

ducking always the touch of must and shall,
whose slippery body is Death's littlest pal,

skilled in quick softness.  Unspontaneous.  cute.

the signal perfume of whose unrepute
focusses in the sweet slow animal
bottomless eyes importantly banal,

Kitty. a whore. Sixteen
                          you corking brute

amused from time to time by clever drolls
fearsomely who do keep their sunday flower.
The babybreasted broad "kitty" twice eight

—beer nothing,the lady'll have a whiskey-sour—

whose least amazing smile is the most great
common divisor of unequal souls.

goodby Betty,don't remember me
pencil your eyes dear and have a good time
with the tall tight boys at Tabari'
s,keep your teeth snowy,stick to beer and lime,
wear dark,and where your meeting breasts are round
have roses darling,it's all i ask of you—
but that when light fails and this sweet profound
Paris moves with lovers,two and two
bound for themselves,when passionately dusk
brings softly down the perfume of the world
(and just as smaller stars begin to husk
heaven)you,you exactly paled and curled

with mystic lips take twilight where i know:
proving to Death that Love is so and so.

# 36

the
nimble
heat
had

long on a certain
taught precarious
holiday
frighteningly

performed
and
at tremont and bromfield i
paused a moment because

on the frying
curb the
quiet face
lay

which had been dorothy
and once
permitted
me for

twenty
iron
men
her common purple

soul
the absurd eyelids sulked
enormous
sobs puckered the foolish

breasts the
droll
mouth
wilted

and not old,harry,a
woman in the crowd
whinnied and a man squeezing her
waist said

the cop 's rung for the
wagon but as i was
lifting the horror
of her toylike

head and vainly
tried to
catch one funny
hand opening the hard great

eyes to noone in particular she
gasped almost
loudly
i'm

so
drunG

k,dear

when you rang at Dick Mid's Place
the madam was a bulb stuck in the door.
a fang of wincing gas showed how
hair,in two fists of shrill colour,
clutched the dull volume of her tumbling face
scribbled with a big grin. her sow-
eyes clicking mischief from thick lids.
the chunklike nose on which always the four
tablets of perspiration erectly sitting.
—If they knew you at Dick Mid's
the three trickling chins began to traipse
into the cheeks "eet smeestaire steevensun
kum een,dare ease Bet,an Leelee,an dee beeg wun"
her handless wrists did gooey severe shapes.

# 38

writhe and
gape of tortured

perspective
rasp and graze of splintered

normality
            crackle and
            sag
of planes       clamors of
collision
collapse     As

peacefully,
lifted
into the awful beauty
                        of sunset

                        the young city
putting off dimension with a blush
enters
the becoming garden of her agony

the bigness of cannon
is skilful,

but i have seen
death's clever enormous voice
which hides in a fragility
of poppies....

i say that sometimes
on these long talkative animals
are laid fists of huger silence.

I have seen all the silence
filled with vivid noiseless boys

at Roupy
i have seen
between barrages,

the night utter ripe unspeaking girls.

# 40

somebody knew Lincoln somebody Xerxes

this man:a narrow thudding timeshaped face
plus innocuous winking hands,carefully
inhabits number 1 on something street

Spring comes
              the lean and definite houses

are troubled.  A sharp blue day
fills with peacefully leaping air
the minute mind of the world.
The lean and

definite houses are
troubled.in the sunset their chimneys converse
angrily,their
roofs are nervous with the soft furious
light,and while fire-escapes and
roofs and chimneys and while roofs and fire-escapes and
chimneys and while chimneys and fire-escapes
and roofs are talking rapidly all together there happens
Something,and They

cease(and
one by one are turned suddenly and softly
into irresponsible toys.)
                          when this man with

the brittle legs winces
swiftly out of number 1 someThing
street and trickles carefully into the park
sits

Down.   pigeons circle
around and around and around the

irresponsible toys
circle wildly in the slow-ly-in creasing fragility
—.Dogs
bark
children
play
-ing
        Are

in the beautiful nonsense of twilight

and somebody Napoleon

# 41

between nose-red gross
walls      sprawling with tipsy
tables the abominable
floor belches smoky

laughter into the filigree
frame of a microscopic
stage whose jouncing curtain.      ,rises
upon one startling doll

undressed in unripe green with
nauseous spiderlegs
and excremental
hair and the eyes of the mother of

god who spits seeds of dead
song about home and love from her
transfigured face a queer
pulp of ecstasy

while in the battered
bodies the odd unlovely
souls struggle      slowly      and      writhe
like caught.brave:flies;

# 42

the rose
is dying the
lips of an old man murder

the petals
hush
mysteriously
invisible mourners move
with prose faces and sobbing,garments
The symbol of the rose

motionless
with grieving feet and
wings
mounts

against the margins of steep song
a stallion sweetness      ,the

lips of an old man murder

the petals.

# 43

it may not always be so;and i say
that if your lips,which i have loved,should touch
another's,and your dear strong fingers clutch
his heart,as mine in time not far away;
if on another's face your sweet hair lay
in such a silence as i know,or such
great writhing words as,uttering overmuch,
stand helplessly before the spirit at bay;

if this should be,i say if this should be—
you of my heart,send me a little word;
that i may go unto him,and take his hands,
saying,Accept all happiness from me.
Then shall i turn my face,and hear one bird
sing terribly afar in the lost lands.

# 44

---

yours is the music for no instrument
yours the preposterous colour unbeheld

—mine the unbought contemptuous intent
till this our flesh merely shall be excelled
by speaking flower
                    (if i have made songs

it does not greatly matter to the sun,
nor will rain care
                    cautiously who prolongs
unserious twilight)Shadows have begun

the hair's worm huge,ecstatic,rathe....

yours are the poems i do not write.

In this at least we have got a bulge on death,
silence,and the keenly musical light

of sudden nothing....la bocca mia "he
kissed wholly trembling"

                    or so thought the lady.

# 45

a thing most new complete fragile intense,
which wholly trembling memory undertakes
—your kiss,the little pushings of flesh,makes
my body sorry when the minute moon
is a remarkable splinter in the quick
of twilight
                ....or if sunset utters one
unhurried muscled huge chromatic
fist skilfully modeling silence
—to feel how through the stopped entire day
horribly and seriously thrills
the moment of enthusiastic space
is a little wonderful,and say
Perhaps her body touched me;and to face

suddenly the lighted living hills

# 46

---

my love is building a building
around you,a frail slippery
house,a strong fragile house
(beginning at the singular beginning

of your smile)a skilful uncouth
prison,a precise clumsy
prison(building thatandthis into Thus,
Around the reckless magic of your mouth)

my love is building a magic,a discrete
tower of magic and(as i guess)

when Farmer Death(whom fairies hate)shall

crumble the mouth-flower fleet
He'll not my tower,
                  laborious,casual

where the surrounded smile
                        hangs

                              breathless

# 47

notice the convulsed orange inch of moon
perching on this silver minute of evening.

We'll choose the way to the forest—no offense
to you,white town whose spires softly dare.
Will take the houseless wisping rune
of road lazily carved on sharpening air.

Fields lying miraculous in violent silence

fill with microscopic whithering
...(that's the Black People,chérie,
who live under stones.) Don't be afraid

and we will pass the simple ugliness
of exact tombs,where a large road crosses
and all the people are minutely dead.

Then you will slowly kiss me

*&*

———————

POEMS 48 TO 96

# 48

her
flesh
Came
at

meassandca V
                    ingint
                              oA
chute

        i had cement for her,
        merrily
we became each
other humped to tumbling

garble    when
a
minute
pulled the sluice

                    emerging.


concrete

raise the shade
will youse dearie?
rain
wouldn't that

get yer goat but
we don't care do
we dearie we should
worry about the rain

huh
dearie?
yknow
i'm

sorry for awl the
poor girls that
gets up god
knows when every

day of their
lives
aint you,

              oo-oo.    dearie

not so
hard dear

you're killing me

# 50

her careful distinct sex whose sharp lips comb

my mumbling gropeofstrength(staggered by the lug
of love)
       sincerely greets,with an occult shrug
asking Through her Muteness will slowly roam
my dumbNess?

       her other,wet,warm

lips limp,across my bruising smile;
as rapidly upon the jiggled norm

of agony my grunting eyes pin tailored flames
Her being at this instant commits

an impenetrable transparency.
the harsh erecting breasts and uttering tits
punish my hug
       presto!

       the bright rile
of jovial hair extremely frames

the face in a hoop of grim ecstasy

# 51

---

between the breasts
of bestial
Marj lie large
men who praise

Marj's cleancornered strokable
body      these men's
fingers toss trunks
shuffle sacks spin kegs they

curl
loving
around
beers

    the world has
these men's hands but their
bodies big and boozing
belong to

Marj
the greenslim purse of whose
face opens
on a fatgold

grin
hooray
hoorah for the large
men who lie

between the breasts
of bestial Marj
for the strong men
who

sleep between the legs of Lil

# 52

ta
ppin
g
toe

hip
popot
amus Back

gen
teel-ly
lugu-
bri ous

                   eyes
LOOPTHELOOP

as

fathandsbangrag

god pity me whom(god distinctly has)
the weightless svelt drifting sexual feather
of your shall i say body?follows
truly through a dribbling moan of jazz

whose arched occasional steep youth swallows
curvingly the keenness of my hips;
or,your first twitch of crisp boy flesh dips
my height in a firm fragile stinging weather,

(breathless with sharp necessary lips)kid

female cracksman of the nifty,ruffian-rogue,
laughing body with wise breasts half-grown,
lisping flesh quick to thread the fattish drone
of I Want a Doll,
                        wispish-agile feet with slid
steps parting the tousle of saxophonic brogue.

# 54

irreproachable ladies firmly lewd
on dangerous slabs of tilting din whose
mouths distinctly walk
                    your smiles accuse

the dusk with an untimid svelt subdued
magic
            while in your eyes there lives
a green egyptian noise. ladies with whom time

feeds especially his immense lips

On whose deep nakedness death most believes,
perpetual girls marching to love

whose bodies kiss me with the square crime
of life....Cecile,the oval shove
of hiding pleasure.  Alice,stinging quips
of flesh.  Loretta,cut the comedy
kid....

        Fran Mag Glad Dorothy

# 55

twentyseven bums give a prostitute the once
-over. fiftythree(and one would see if it could)

eyes say the breasts look very good:
firmlysquirmy with a slight jounce,

thirteen pants have a hunch

admit in threedimensional distress
these hips were made for Horizontal Business
(set on big legs nice to pinch

assiduously which justgraze
each other).   As the lady lazily struts

                                   (her
thickish flesh superior to the genuine daze
of unmarketable excitation,

whose careless movements carefully scatter

pink propaganda of annihilation.

# 56

Babylon slim
-ness of
evenslicing
eyes are chisels

scarlet Goes
with her
whitehot
face,gashed

by hair's blue cold

jolts of
lovecrazed abrupt

flesh split "Pretty
Baby"
to
numb rhythm before christ

she sits dropping on a caret of clenched arms
a delicately elephantine face
(It is necessary to find Hassan's Place
by tiny streets shrugging with colour)
the mouth who sits between her cheeks
utters a thud of scarlet. always.   More
interesting,as i think,her charms
en repos....a fattish leg leaks
obscenely from the dress.   one nipple tries.
playfully to peek into the belly
whose deep squirm nibbles. another couches,
weary,upon a flabby mattress of jelly....
than when to the kanoon she totters,slouches,
with giggling hips and frozen eyes

# 58

here is little Effie's head
whose brains are made of gingerbread
when the judgment day comes
God will find six crumbs

stooping by the coffinlid
waiting for something to rise
as the other somethings did—
you imagine His surprise

bellowing through the general noise
Where is Effie who was dead?
—to God in a tiny voice,
i am may the first crumb said

whereupon its fellow five
crumbs chuckled as if they were alive
and number two took up the song,
might i'm called and did no wrong

cried the third crumb,i am should
and this is my little sister could
with our big brother who is would
don't punish us for we were good;

and the last crumb with some shame
whispered unto God,my name
is must and with the others i've
been Effie who isn't alive

just imagine it I say
God amid a monstrous din
watch your step and follow me
stooping by Effie's little,in

(want a match or can you see?)
which the six subjunctive crumbs
twitch like mutilated thumbs:
picture His peering biggest whey

coloured face on which a frown
puzzles,but I know the way—
(nervously Whose eyes approve
the blessed while His ears are crammed

with the strenuous music of
the innumerable capering damned)
—staring wildly up and down
the here we are now judgment day

cross the threshold have no dread
lift the sheet back in this way.
here is little Effie's head
whose brains are made of gingerbread

# 59

of this wilting wall the colour drub
souring sunbeams,of a foetal fragrance
to rickety unclosed blinds inslants
peregrinate,a cigar-stub
disintegrates,above,underdrawers club
the faintly sweating air with pinkness,
one pale dog behind a slopcaked shrub
painstakingly utters a slippery mess,
a star sleepily,feebly,scratches the sore
of morning.  But i am interested more
intricately in the delicate scorn
with which in a putrid window every day
almost leans a lady whose still-born
smile involves the comedy of decay,

# 60

the bed is not very big

a sufficient pillow shoveling
her small manure-shaped head

one sheet on which distinctly wags

at times the weary twig
of a neckless nudity
(very occasionally budding

a flabby algebraic odour

jigs
    et tout en face
always wiggles the perfectly dead
finger of thitherhithering gas.

clothed with a luminous fur

poilu

    a Jesus sags
in frolicsome wooden agony).

# 61

in making Marjorie god hurried
a boy's body on unsuspicious
legs of girl. his left hand quarried
the quartzlike face. his right slapped
the amusing big vital vicious
vegetable of her mouth.
Upon the whole he suddenly clapped
a tiny sunset of vermouth
-colour.   Hair. he put between
her lips a moist mistake,whose fragrance hurls
me into tears,as the dusty new-
ness of her obsolete gaze begins to.   lean....
a little against me,when for two
dollars i fill her hips with boys and girls

# 62

---

fabulous against   ,a,fathoming jelly
of vital futile huge light as she
does not stand-ing.unsits

                     her(wrist
performs a thundering trivial)it.y

protuberant through the room's skilful of thing
silent spits discrete lumps of noise....
furniture

              unsolemnly  :bur  sting
the skinfull of Ludicrous,solidity which a.   ,kissed
with is nearness.)peers:body of

                              aching toys
in unsmooth sexual luminosity spree.

—dear)the   uncouthly Her.thuglike stare the
pollenizing vacancy
when,Thy patters?hands....is swig

it does who eye     sO neatly big

# 63

the dirty colours of her kiss have just
throttled
          my seeing blood,her heart's chatter

riveted a weeping skyscraper

in me

     i bite on the eyes' brittle crust
(only feeling the belly's merry thrust
Boost my huge passion like a business

and the Y her legs panting as they press

proffers its omelet of fluffy lust)
at six exactly
               the alarm tore

two slits in her cheeks.  A brain peered at the dawn.
she got up

          with a gashing yellow yawn
and tottered to a glass bumping things.
she picked wearily something from the floor

Her hair was mussed,and she coughed while tying strings

the dress was a suspicious madder,importing the cruelty of roses.  The exciting simplicity of her hipless body,pausing to invent imperceptible bulgings of the pretended breasts,forked in surprisable unliving eyes chopped by a swollen inanity of picture hat.

the arms hung ugly.,the hands sharp and impertinently dead.

expression began with the early cessation of her skirt. fleshless melody of the,keenly lascivious legs.  painful ankles large acute brutal feet propped on irrelevantly ferocious heels.

Her gasping slippery body moved with the hideous spontaneity of a solemn mechanism.  beneath her drab tempo of hasteful futility lived brilliantly the enormous rhythm of absurdity.

skin like the poisonous fragility of ice newly formed upon an old pool.  Her nose was small,exact,stupid. mouth normal,large,unclever.  hair genuinely artificial, unpleasantly tremendous.

under flat lusts of light her nice concupiscence appeared rounded.

if she were alive,death was amusing

# 65

---

Dick Mid's large bluish face without eyebrows

sits in the kitchen nights and chews a two-bit
cigar
     waiting for the bulls to pull his joint.
Jimmie was a dude.  Dark hair and nice hands.

with a little eye that rolled and made its point

Jimmie's sister worked for Dick.  And had some rows
over percent.  The gang got shot up twice,it
operated in the hundred ands

All the chips would kid Jimmie to give them a kiss
but Jimmie lived regular. stewed three times a week.
and slept twice a week with a big toothless girl
in Yonkers.
     Dick Mid's green large three teeth leak

smoke:remembering,two pink big lips curl....

how Jimmie was framed and got his

# 66

---

my girl's tall with hard long eyes
as she stands,with her long hard hands keeping
silence on her dress,good for sleeping
is her long hard body filled with surprise
like a white shocking wire,when she smiles
a hard long smile it sometimes makes
gaily go clean through me tickling aches,
and the weak noise of her eyes easily files
my impatience to an edge—my girl's tall
and taut,with thin legs just like a vine
that's spent all of its life on a garden-wall,
and is going to die.  When we grimly go to bed
with these legs she begins to heave and twine
about me,and to kiss my face and head.

Paris;this April sunset completely utters
utters serenely silently a cathedral

before whose upward lean magnificent face
the streets turn young with rain,

spiral acres of bloated rose
coiled within cobalt miles of sky
yield to and heed
the mauve
        of twilight(who slenderly descends,
daintily carrying in her eyes the dangerous first stars)
people move love hurry in a gently

arriving gloom and
see!(the new moon
fills abruptly with sudden silver
these torn pockets of lame and begging colour)while
there and here the lithe indolent prostitute
Night,argues

with certain houses

# 68

impossibly

motivated by midnight
the flyspecked abdominous female
indubitably tellurian
strolls
        emitting minute grins

each an intaglio.
Nothing
has also carved upon her much

too white forehead a pair of
eyes which mutter thickly(as one merely
terricolous American an instant doubts
the authenticity

of these antiquities—relaxing
                                hurries
elsewhere;to blow

incredible wampum

# 69

little ladies more
than dead exactly dance
in my head,precisely
dance where danced la guerre.

Mimi à
la voix fragile
qui chatouille Des
Italiens

the putain with the ivory throat
Marie Louise Lallemand
n'est-ce pas que je suis belle
chéri? les anglais m'aiment
tous,les américains
aussi...."bon dos,bon cul de Paris"(Marie
Vierge
Priez
Pour
Nous)

with the
long lips of
Lucienne which dangle
the old men and hot
men se promènent
doucement le soir(ladies

accurately dead les anglais
sont gentils et les américains
aussi,ils payent bien les américains dance

exactly in my brain voulez-
vous coucher avec
moi? Non? pourquoi?

ladies skilfully
dead precisely dance
where has danced la
guerre j'm'appelle
Manon,cinq rue Henri Mounier
voulez-vous coucher avec moi?
te ferai Mimi
te ferai Minette,
dead exactly dance
si vous voulez
chatouiller
mon lézard ladies suddenly
j'm'en fous de nègres

                  (in the twilight of Paris
Marie Louise with queenly
legs cinq rue Henri
Mounier a little love
begs,Mimi with the body
like une boîte à joujoux,want nice sleep?
toutes les petites femmes exactes
qui dansent toujours in my
head dis-donc,Paris

ta gorge mystérieuse
pourquoi se promène-t-elle,pourquoi
éclate ta voix
fragile couleur de pivoine?)
                  with the

long lips of Lucienne which
dangle the old men and hot men
precisely dance in my head
ladies carefully dead

# 70

---

nearer:breath of my breath:take not thy tingling
limbs from me:make my pain their crazy meal
letting thy tigers of smooth sweetness steal
slowly in dumb blossoms of new mingling:
deeper:blood of my blood:with upwardcringing
swiftness plunge these leopards of white dream
in the glad flesh of my fear:more neatly ream
this pith of darkness:carve an evilfringing
flower of madness on gritted lips
and on sprawled eyes squirming with light insane
chisel the killing flame that dizzily grips.

Querying greys between mouthed houses curl

thirstily.  Dead stars stink.  dawn.  Inane,

the poetic carcass of a girl

# 71

the poem her belly marched through me as
one army.   From her nostrils to her feet

she smelled of silence.   The inspired cleat

of her glad leg pulled into a sole mass
my separate lusts
                    her hair was like a gas
evil to feel.   Unwieldy....


                        the bloodbeat
in her fierce laziness tried to repeat
a trick of syncopation Europe has

—. One day i felt a mountain touch me where
i stood (maybe nine miles off).   It was spring

sun-stirring.   sweetly to the mangling air
muchness of buds mattered.   a valley spilled
its tickling river in my eyes,
                        the killed

world wriggled like a twitched string.

when the spent day begins to frail
(whose grave already three or two
young stars with spades of silver dig)

by beauty i declare to you

if what i am at one o'clock
to little lips(which have not sinned
in whose displeasure lives a kiss)
kneeling,your frequent mercy begs,

sharply believe me,wholly,well
—did(wisely suddenly into
a dangerous womb of cringing air)
the largest hour push deep his din

of wallowing male(shock beyond shock
blurted)strokes,vibrant with the purr
of echo pouring in a mesh
of following tone:did this and this

spire strike midnight(and did occur
bell beyond fiercely spurting bell
a jetted music splashing fresh
upon silence)i without fail

entered became and was these twin
imminent lisping bags of flesh;
became eyes moist lithe shuddering big,
the luminous laughter,and the legs

whereas,at twenty minutes to

one,i am this blueeyed Finn
emerging from a lovehouse who
buttons his coat against the wind

# 73

---

who knows if the moon's
a balloon,coming out of a keen city
in the sky—filled with pretty people?
(and if you and i should

get into it,if they
should take me and take you into their balloon,
why then
we'd go up higher with all the pretty people

than houses and steeples and clouds:
go sailing
away and away sailing into a keen
city which nobody's ever visited,where

always
        it's
            Spring)and everyone's
in love and flowers pick themselves

# 74

inthe,exquisite;

morning    sure    lyHer eye s exactly sit,ata little roundtable
among otherlittle roundtables  Her,eyes    count   slow(ly

obstre peroustimidi ties surElyfl)oat   iNg,the

ofpieces ofof sunligh tof fa l l in gof throughof treesOf.

(Fields Elysian

the like,a)slEEping neck a breathing a   ,lies
(slo wlythe wom an pa)ris her
flesh:wakes
              in little streets

while exactlygir lisHlegs;play;ing;nake;D
and

chairs wait under the trees

Fields slowly Elysian in
a firmcool-Ness      taxis, s.QuirM

and,   b etw ee nch air st ott er s thesillyold
WomanSellingBalloonS

In theex qui site

morning,
        her sureLyeye s sit-ex actly her sitsat a surely!little,
roundtable amongother;littleexactly round.  tables,

Her
    .eyes

# 75

Spring is like a perhaps hand
(which comes carefully
out of Nowhere)arranging
a window,into which people look(while
people stare
arranging and changing placing
carefully there a strange
thing and a known thing here)and

changing everything carefully

spring is like a perhaps
Hand in a window
(carefully to
and fro moving New and
Old things,while
people stare carefully
moving a perhaps
fraction of flower here placing
an inch of air there)and

without breaking anything.

# 76

riverly is a flower
gone softly by tomb
rosily gods whiten
befall saith rain

anguish
of dream-send is
hushed
in

moan-loll where
night      gathers
morte carved smiles

cloud-gloss is at moon-cease
soon
verbal mist-flowers close
ghosts on prowl gorge

sly slim gods stare

the wind is a Lady with
bright slender eyes(who

moves)at sunset
and who—touches—the
hills without any reason

(i have spoken with this
indubitable and green person "Are
You the wind?" "Yes" "why do you touch flowers
as if they were unalive,as

if They were ideas?" "because,sir
things which in my mind blossom will
stumble beneath a clumsiest disguise,appear
capable of fragility and indecision

—do not suppose these
without any reason and otherwise
roses and mountains
different from the i am who wanders

imminently across the renewed world"
to me said the)wind being A lady in a green
dress,who;touches:the fields
(at sunset)

                    (one!)
the wisti-twisti barber
-pole is climbing

people high,up-in

tenements talk.in sawdust Voices
                    a:whispering drunkard passes

gee i like to think of dead it means nearer because deeper
firmer since darker than little round water at one end of
the well  it's too cool to be crooked and it's too firm to be
hard but it's sharp and thick and it loves,  every old thing
falls in rosebugs and jackknives and kittens and pennies
they all sit there looking at each other having the fastest
time because they've never met before

dead's more even than how many ways of sitting on your
head your unnatural hair has in the morning

dead's clever too like POF goes the alarm off and the little
striker having the best time tickling away everybody's
brain so everybody just puts out their finger and they stuff
the poor thing all full of fingers

dead has a smile like the nicest man you've never met who
maybe winks at you in a streetcar and you pretend you
don't but really you do see and you are My how glad he
winked and hope he'll do it again

or if it talks about you somewhere behind your back it
makes your neck feel pleasant and stoopid  and if dead
says may i have this one and was never introduced you say
Yes because you know you want it to dance with you and
it wants to and it can dance and Whocares

dead's fine like hands do you see that water flowerpots in
windows but they live higher in their house than you so
that's all you see but you don't want to

dead's happy like the way underclothes All so differently
solemn and inti and sitting on one string

dead never says my dear,Time for your musiclesson and
you like music and to have somebody play who can but
you know you never can and why have to?

dead's nice like a dance where you danced simple hours
and you take all your prickley-clothes off and squeeze-
into-largeness without one word   and you lie still as
anything  in largeness and this largeness begins to give
you,the dance all over again and you,feel all again all over
the way men you liked made you feel when they touched
you(but that's not all)because largeness tells you so you
can feel what you made,men feel when,you touched,them

dead's sorry like a thistlefluff-thing which goes landing
away all by himself on somebody's roof or something
where who-ever-heard-of-growing and nobody expects
you to anyway

dead says come with me he says(andwhyevernot)into the
round well and see the kitten and the penny and the
jackknife and the rosebug
                          and you say Sure you say
(like that) sure i'll come with you you say for i like
kittens i do and jackknives i do and pennies i do and
rosebugs i do

suppose
Life is an old man carrying flowers on his head.

young death sits in a café
smiling,a piece of money held between
his thumb and first finger

(i say "will he buy flowers" to you
and "Death is young
life wears velour trousers
life totters,life has a beard" i

say to you who are silent.—"Do you see
Life?he is there and here,
or that,or this
or nothing or an old man 3 thirds
asleep,on his head
flowers,always crying
to nobody something about les
roses les bluets
                    yes,
                        will He buy?
Les belles bottes—oh hear
,pas chères")

and my love slowly answered I think so.   But
I think I see someone else

there is a lady,whose name is Afterwards
she is sitting beside young death,is slender;
likes flowers.

# 81

```
                          i will be
M o ving in the Street of her

bodyfee l inga ro undMe the traffic of
lovely;muscles-sinke x p i r i n    g S
     uddenl
Y            totouch
                     the curvedship of
                                    Her-
....kIss     her:hands
                    will play on,mE as
dea d tunes OR s-cra p-y leaVes flut te rin g
from Hideous trees or

     Maybe Mandolins
                      l oo k-
     pigeons fly ingand

whee(:are,SpRiN,k,LiNg an in-stant with sunLight
t h e n)l-
ing all go BlacK wh-eel-ing

oh
   ver
        mYveRylitTle

street
where
you will come,

                 at twi li ght
     s(oon & there's
     a            m oo
)n.
```

of this sunset(which is so
filled with fear people bells)i
say your eyes can take
day away more softly horribly suddenly;

(of these two most
early stars wincing upon a single
colour,i know only that your hands
move more simply upon the evening

and à propos such light and shape as means
the moon,i somehow feel
your smile slightly is a more
minute adventure)

lady.   The clumsy dark threatens(and i do
not speak nor think nor am aware
of anything
                save that these houses bulge
like memories in one crooked street

of a mind peacefully and skilfully which is disappearing

# 83

Take for example this:

if to the colour of midnight
to a more than darkness(which
is myself and Paris and all
things)the bright
rain
occurs deeply,beautifully

and i(being at a window
in this midnight)
                    for no reason feel
deeply completely conscious of the rain or rather
Somebody who uses roofs and streets skilfully to make a
possible and beautiful sound:

if a(perhaps)clock strikes,in the alive
coolness,very faintly and
finally through altogether delicate gestures of rain

a colour comes,which is morning,O do not wonder that

(just at the edge of day)i surely
make a millionth poem which will not wholly
miss you;or if i certainly create,lady,
one of the thousand selves who are your smile.

# 84

before the fragile gradual throne of night
slowly when several stars are opening
one beyond one immaculate curving
cool treasures of silence
                              (slenderly wholly
rising,herself uprearing wholly slowly,
lean in the hips and her sails filled with dream—
when on a green brief gesture of twilight
trembles the imagined galleon of Spring)

somewhere unspeaking sits my life;the grim
clenched mind of me somewhere begins again,
shares the year's perfect agony.   Waiting

(always)upon a fragile instant when

herself me(slowly,wholly me)will press
in the young lips unearthly slenderness

# 85

the ivory performing rose

of you,worn upon my mind
all night,quitting only in the unkind

dawn its muscle amorous

pricks with minute odour these gross
days
        when i think of you and do not live:
and the empty twilight cannot grieve
nor the autumn,as i grieve,faint for your face

O stay with me slightly.  or until

with neat obscure obvious hands

Time stuff the sincere stomach of each mill

of the ingenious gods.(i am punished.
They have stolen into recent lands
the flower
            with their enormous fingers unwished

utterly and amusingly i am pash
possibly because
                    .dusk and if it
perhaps drea-mingly Is(not-
quite trees hugging with the rash,
coherent light
                )only to trace with
stiffening slow shrill eyes beyond a fit-
and-cling of stuffs the alert willing myth
of body,which will make oddly to strut
my indolent priceless smile,
                        until
this very frail enormous star(do you see
it?)and this shall dance upon the nude
and final silence and shall the
(i do but touch you)timid lewd
moon plunge skilfully into the hill.

# 87

when my love comes to see me it's
just a little like music,a
little more like curving colour(say
orange)
        against silence,or darkness....

the coming of my love emits
a wonderful smell in my mind,

you should see when i turn to find
her how my least heart-beat becomes less.
And then all her beauty is a vise

whose stilling lips murder suddenly me,

but of my corpse the tool her smile makes something
suddenly luminous and precise

—and then we are I and She....

what is that the hurdy-gurdy's playing

# 88

---

the mind is its own beautiful prisoner.
Mine looked long at the sticky moon
opening in dusk her new wings

then decently hanged himself,one afternoon.

The last thing he saw was you
naked amid unnaked things,

your flesh,a succinct wandlike animal,
a little strolling with the futile purr
of blood;your sex squeaked like a billiard-cue
chalking itself,as not to make an error,
with twists spontaneously methodical.
He suddenly tasted worms windows and roses

he laughed,and closed his eyes as a girl closes
her left hand upon a mirror.

# 89

let's live suddenly without thinking

under honest trees,
                    a stream
does.the brain of cleverly-crinkling
-water pursues the angry dream
of the shore.  By midnight,
                    a moon
scratches the skin of the organised hills

an edged nothing begins to prune

let's live like the light that kills
and let's as silence,
                    because Whirl's after all:
(after me)love,and after you.
I occasionally feel vague how
vague i don't know tenuous Now-
spears and The Then-arrows making do
our mouths something red,something tall

# 90

---

i have loved,let us see if that's all.
Bit into you as teeth,in the stone
of a musical fruit.  My lips pleasantly groan
on your taste.  Jumped the quick wall

of your smile into stupid gardens
if this were not enough(not really enough
pulled one before one the vague tough

exquisite

      flowers,whom hardens
richly,darkness.  On the whole
possibly have i loved....?you)
                    sheath before sheath

stripped to the Odour.  (and here's what WhoEver will know
Had you as bite teeth;
i stood with you as a foal

stands but as the trees,lay,which grow

# 91

my sonnet is A light goes on in
the toiletwindow,that's straightacross from
my window,night air bothered with a rustling din

sort of sublimated tom-tom
which quite outdoes the mandolin-

man's tiny racket.   The horses sleep upstairs.
And you can see their ears.   Ears win-

k,funny stable.   In the morning they go out in pairs:
amazingly,one pair is white
(but you know that)they look at each other.   Nudge.

(if they love each other,who cares?)
They pull the morning out of the night.

I am living with a mouse who shares

my meals with him,which is fair as i judge.

and this day it was Spring....us
drew lewdly the murmurous minute clumsy
smelloftheworld.  We intricately
alive,cleaving the luminous stammer of bodies
(eagerly just not each other touch)seeking,some
street which easily trickles a brittle fuss
of fragile huge humanity....
                              Numb
thoughts,kicking in the rivers of our blood,miss
by how terrible inches speech—it
made you a little dizzy did the world's smell
(but i was thinking why the girl-and-bird
of you move....moves....and also,i'll admit—)

till,at the corner of Nothing and Something,we heard
a handorgan in twilight playing like hell

# 93

i have found what you are like
the rain,

      (Who feathers frightened fields
with the superior dust-of-sleep. wields

easily the pale club of the wind
and swirled justly souls of flower strike

the air in utterable coolness

deeds of green thrilling light
               with thinned
newfragile yellows

          lurch and.press
—in the woods
        which
           stutter
              and

                  sing
And the coolness of your smile is
stirringofbirds between my arms;but
i should rather than anything
have(almost when hugeness will shut
quietly)almost,
        your kiss

---

if i should sleep with a lady called death
get another man with firmer lips
to take your new mouth in his teeth
(hips pumping pleasure into hips).

Seeing how the limp huddling string
of your smile over his body squirms
kissingly,i will bring you every spring
handfuls of little normal worms.

Dress deftly your flesh in stupid stuffs,
phrase the immense weapon of your hair.
Understanding why his eye laughs,
i will bring you every year

something which is worth the whole,
an inch of nothing for your soul.

# 95

---

it is funny,you will be dead some day.
By you the mouth hair eyes,and i mean
the unique and nervously obscene

need;it's funny.  They will all be dead

knead of lustfulhunched deeplytoplay
lips and stare the gross fuzzy-pash
—dead—and the dark gold delicately smash...
grass,and the stars,of my shoulder in stead.

It is a funny,thing.  And you will be

and i and all the days and nights that matter
knocked by sun moon jabbed jerked with ecstasy
....tremble(not knowing how much better

than me will you like the rain's face and

the rich improbable hands of the Wind)

# 96

---

i like my body when it is with your
body.   It is so quite new a thing.
Muscles better and nerves more.
i like your body.   i like what it does,
i like its hows.   i like to feel the spine
of your body and its bones,and the trembling
-firm-smooth ness and which i will
again and again and again
kiss,   i like kissing this and that of you,
i like,slowly stroking the,shocking fuzz
of your electric fur,and what-is-it comes
over parting flesh....And eyes big love-crumbs,

and possibly i like the thrill

of under me you so quite new

# XLI Poems

---

POEMS 97 TO 121

conversation with my friend is particularly

to enjoy the composed sudden body atop which always quivers the electric Distinct face haughtily vital clinched in a swoon of synopsis

despite a sadistic modesty his mind is seen frequently fingering the exact beads of a faultless languor when invisibly consult with some delicious image the a little strolling lips and eyes inwardly crisping

for my friend,feeling is the sacred and agonizing proximity to its desire of a doomed impetuous acute sentience whose whitehot lips however suddenly approached may never quite taste the wine which their nearness evaporates

to think is the slippery contours of a vase inexpressibly fragile it is for the brain irrevocably frigid to touch a merest shape which however slenderly by it caressed will explode and spill the immediate imperceptible content

my friend's being,out of the spontaneous clumsy trivial acrobatic edgeless gesture of existence,continually whittles keen careful futile flowers

(isolating with perpetually meticulous concupiscence the bright large undeniable disease of Life,himself occasionally contrives an unreal precise intrinsic fragment of actuality),

an orchid whose velocity is sculptural

# 98

---

the skinny voice

of the leatherfaced
woman with the crimson
nose and coquettishly-
cocked bonnet

having ceased      the

captain
announces that as three
dimes seven nickels and ten
pennies have been deposited upon

the drum   there is need

of just twenty five cents
dear friends
to make it an even
dollar      whereupon

the Divine Average who was

attracted by the inspired
sister's howling moves
off
will anyone tell him why he should

blow two bits for the coming of Christ Jesus

?
??
???
!

nix,kid

# 99

---

the
    sky
        was
can  dy  lu
minous
        edible
spry
    pinks shy
lemons
greens  coo  l choc
olate
s.

  un  der,
  a  lo
co
mo
    tive    s  pout
                ing
                  vi
                  o
                lets

# 100

---

when i am in Boston,i do not speak.
and i sit in the click of ivory balls....

noting flies,which jerk upon the weak
colour of table-cloths,the electric When
In Doubt Buy Of(but a roof hugs
whom)
        as the august evening mauls
Kneeland,and a waiter cleverly lugs
indigestible honeycake to men
....one perfectly smooth coffee
tasting of hellas,i drink,or sometimes two
remarking cries of paklavah meeah.
(Very occasionally three.)
and i gaze on the cindercoloured little ΜΕΓΑ
ΕΛΛΗΝΙΚΟΝ ΞΕΝΟΔΟΧΕΙΟΝ ΤΠΝΟΤ

# 101

Humanity i love you
because you would rather black the boots of
success than enquire whose soul dangles from his
watch-chain which would be embarrassing for both

parties and because you
unflinchingly applaud all
songs containing the words country home and
mother when sung at the old howard

Humanity i love you because
when you're hard up you pawn your
intelligence to buy a drink and when
you're flush pride keeps

you from the pawn shop and
because you are continually committing
nuisances but more
especially in your own house

Humanity i love you because you
are perpetually putting the secret of
life in your pants and forgetting
it's there and sitting down

on it
and because you are
forever making poems in the lap
of death Humanity

i hate you

# 102

---

between green
                    mountains
sings the flinger
of

fire   beyond red rivers
of fair perpetual
feet the
sinuous

          riot

the
flashing
bacchant.

partedpetaled
mouth,face
delirious.  indivisible
grace

       of dancing

# 103

Picasso
you give us Things
which
bulge:grunting lungs pumped full of sharp thick mind

you make us shrill
presents always
shut in the sumptuous screech of
simplicity

(out of the
black unbunged
Something gushes vaguely a squeak of planes
or

between squeals of
Nothing grabbed with circular shrieking tightness
solid screams whisper.)
Lumberman of The Distinct

your brain's
axe only chops hugest inherent
Trees of Ego,from
whose living and biggest

bodies lopped
of every
prettiness

you hew form truly

# 104

little tree
little silent Christmas tree
you are so little
you are more like a flower

who found you in the green forest
and were you very sorry to come away?
see      i will comfort you
because you smell so sweetly

i will kiss your cool bark
and hug you safe and tight
just as your mother would,
only don't be afraid

look      the spangles
that sleep all the year in a dark box
dreaming of being taken out and allowed to shine,
the balls the chains red and gold the fluffy threads

put up your little arms
and i'll give them all to you to hold
every finger shall have its ring
and there won't be a single place dark or unhappy

then when you're quite dressed
you'll stand in the window for everyone to see
and how they'll stare!
oh but you'll be very proud

and my little sister and i will take hands
and looking up at our beautiful tree
we'll dance and sing
"Noel Noel"

cruelly,love
walk the autumn long;
the last flower in whose hair,
thy lips are cold with songs

for which is
first to wither,to pass?
shallowness of sunlight
falls and,cruelly,
across the grass
Comes the
moon

love,walk the
autumn
love,for the last
flower in the hair withers;
thy hair is acold with
dreams,
love thou art frail

—walk the longness of autumn
smile dustily to the people,
for winter
who crookedly care.

why did you go
little fourpaws?
you forgot to shut
your big eyes.

where did you go?
like little kittens
are all the leaves
which open in the rain.

little kittens who
are called spring,
is what we stroke
maybe asleep?

do you know?or maybe did
something go away
ever so quietly
when we weren't looking.

# 107

into the smiting
sky tense
with
blend

ing
the
tree     leaps
                    a stiffened exquisite

i
wait the sweet
annihilation of swift
flesh

i make me stern against
your charming strength


O haste
          annihilator
drawing into you my enchanting
leaves

when life is quite through with
and leaves say alas,
much is to do
for the swallow,that closes
a flight in the blue;

when love's had his tears out,
perhaps shall pass
a million years
(while a bee dozes
on the poppies,the dears;

when all's done and said,and
under the grass
lies her head
by oaks and roses
deliberated.)

# 109

Lady of Silence
from the winsome cage of
thy body
rose
     through the sensible
night
a
quick bird

(tenderly upon
the dark's prodigious face
thy
voice
     scattering perfume-gifted
wings
suddenly escorts
with feet
sun-sheer

the smarting beauty of dawn)

# 110

when unto nights of autumn do complain
earth's ghastlier trees by whom Time measured is
when frost to dance maketh the sagest pane
of littler huts with peerless fantasies
or the unlovely longness of the year

droops with things dead athwart the narrowing hours
and hope(by cold espoused unto fear)
in dreadful corners hideously cowers—

i do excuse me,love,to Death and Time

storms and rough cold,wind's menace and leaf's grieving:
from the impressed fingers of sublime
Memory,of that loveliness receiving
the image my proud heart cherished as fair.

(The child-head poised with the serious hair)

# 111

---

perhaps it is to feel strike
the silver fish of her nakedness
with fins sharply pleasant,my

youth has travelled toward her these years

or to snare the timid like
of her mind to my mind that i

am come by little countries to the yes

of her youth.
           And if somebody hears
what i say—let him be pitiful:
because i've travelled all alone
through the forest of wonderful,
and that my feet have surely known
the furious ways and the peaceful,

and because she is beautiful

# 112

---

if learned darkness from our searched world

should wrest the rare unwisdom of thy eyes,
and if thy hands flowers of silence curled

upon a wish,to rapture should surprise
my soul slowly which on thy beauty dreams
(proud through the cold perfect night whisperless

to mark,how that asleep whitely she seems

whose lips the whole of life almost do guess)

if god should send the morning;and before
my doubting window leaves softly to stir,
of thoughtful trees whom night hath pondered o'er
—and frailties of dimension to occur

about us
            and birds known,scarcely to sing

(heart,could we bear the marvel of this thing?)

# 113

Where's Madge then,
Madge and her men?
buried with
Alice in her hair,
(but if you ask the rain
he'll not tell where.)

beauty makes terms
with time and his worms,
when loveliness
says sweetly Yes
to wind and cold;
and how much earth
is Madge worth?
Inquire of the flower that sways in the autumn
she will never guess.
but i know

# 114

---

when my sensational moments are no more
unjoyously bullied of vilest mind

and sweet uncaring earth by thoughtful war
heaped wholly with high wilt of human rind—
when over hate has triumphed darkly love

and the small spiritual cry of spring
utters a striving flower,
                                      just where strove
the droll god-beasts

                            do thou distinctly bring
thy footstep,and the rushing of thy deep
hair and the smiting smile didst love to use
in other days (drawing my Mes from sleep
whose stranger dreams thy strangeness must abuse....)

Time being not for us,purple roses were
sweeter to thee
                    perchance to me deeper.

this is the garden:colours come and go,
frail azures fluttering from night's outer wing
strong silent greens serenely lingering,
absolute lights like baths of golden snow.
This is the garden:pursed lips do blow
upon cool flutes within wide glooms,and sing
(of harps celestial to the quivering string)
invisible faces hauntingly and slow.

This is the garden.   Time shall surely reap,
and on Death's blade lie many a flower curled,
in other lands where other songs be sung;
yet stand They here enraptured,as among
the slow deep trees perpetual of sleep
some silver-fingered fountain steals the world.

when the proficient poison of sure sleep
bereaves us of our slow tranquillities

and He without Whose favour nothing is
(being of men called Love) upward doth leap
from the mute hugeness of depriving deep,

with thunder of those hungering wings of His,

into the lucent and large signories
—i shall not smile beloved;i shall not weep:

when from the less-than-whiteness of thy face
(whose eyes inherit vacancy) will time
extract his inconsiderable doom,
when these thy lips beautifully embrace
nothing
       and when thy bashful hands assume

silence beyond the mystery of rhyme

# 117

I have seen her a stealthily frail
flower walking with its fellows in the death
of light,against whose enormous curve of flesh
exactly cubes of tiny fragrance try;
i have watched certain petals rapidly wish
in the corners of her youth;whom,fiercely shy
and gently brutal,the prettiest wrath
of blossoms dishevelling made a pale
fracas upon the accurate moon....
Across the important gardens her body
will come toward me with its hurting sexual smell
of lilies....beyond night's silken immense swoon
the moon is like a floating silver hell
a song of adolescent ivory.

come nothing to my comparable soul
which with existence has conversed in vain,
O scrupulously take thy trivial toll,
for whose cool feet this frantic heart is fain;
try me with thy perfumes which have seduced
the mightier nostrils of the fervent dead,
feed with felicities me wormperused
by whom the hungering mouth of time is fed:
and if i like not what thou givest me
to him let me complain,whose seat is where
revolving planets struggle to be free
with the astounding everlasting air—
but if i like,i'll take between thy hands
what no man feels,no woman understands.

# 119

O Thou to whom the musical white spring

offers her lily inextinguishable,
taught by thy tremulous grace bravely to fling

Implacable death's mysteriously sable
robe from her redolent shoulders,
                                    Thou from whose
feet reincarnate song suddenly leaping
flameflung,mounts,inimitably to lose
herself where the wet stars softly are keeping

their exquisite dreams—O Love! upon thy dim
shrine of intangible commemoration,
(from whose faint close as some grave languorous hymn

pledged to illimitable dissipation
unhurried clouds of incense fleetly roll)

i spill my bright incalculable soul.

# 120

---

and what were roses.   Perfume?for i do
forget....or mere Music mounting unsurely

twilight
          but here were something more maturely
childish,more beautiful almost than you.

Yet if not flower,tell me softly who

be these haunters of dreams always demurely
halfsmiling from cool faces,moving purely
with muted step,yet somewhat proudly too—

are they not ladies,ladies of my dreams
justly touching roses their fingers whitely
live by?
          or better,
                         queens,queens laughing lightly
crowned with far colours,

                              thinking very much
of nothing and whom dawn loves most to touch

wishing by willows,bending upon streams?

# 121

---

who's most afraid of death?thou

                                 art of him
utterly afraid,i love of thee
(beloved)this

           and truly i would be
near when his scythe takes crisply the whim
of thy smoothness. and mark the fainting
murdered petals. with the caving stem.

But of all most would i be one of them

round the hurt heart which do so frailly cling....)
i who am but imperfect in my fear

Or with thy mind against my mind,to hear
nearing our hearts' irrevocable play—
through the mysterious high futile day

an enormous stride
                    (and drawing thy mouth toward

my mouth,steer our lost bodies carefully downward)

# is 5

POEMS 122 TO 189

# 122

with breathing as(faithfully)her lownecked
dress a little topples and slightly expands

one square foot mired in silk wrinkling loth
stocking begins queerly to do a few
gestures to death,
                    the silent shoulders are both
slowly with pinkish ponderous arms bedecked
whose white thick wrists deliver promptly to
a deep lap enormous mindless hands.
and no one knows what(i am sure of this)
her blunt unslender,what her big unkeen

"Business is rotten" the face yawning said

what her mouth thinks of
                         (if it were a kiss
distinct entirely melting sinuous lean...
whereof this lady in some book had read

## II. MAME

she puts down the handmirror.  "Look at" arranging
before me a mellifluous idiot grin
(with what was nose upwrinkled into nothing
earthly,while the slippery eyes drown
in surging flesh).  A thumblike index down-
dragging yanks back skin "see"(i,seeing,ceased
to breathe).  The plump left fist opening
"wisdom."  Flicker of gold.  "Yep.  No gas.  Flynn"

the words drizzle untidily from released
cheeks "I'll tell duh woild;some noive all right.
Aint much on looks but how dat baby ached."

and when i timidly hinted "novocaine?"
the eyes outstart,curl,bloat,are newly baked

and swaggering cookies of indignant light

### III. GERT

joggle i think will do it although the glad
monosyllable jounce possibly can tell
better how the balloons move(as
her ghost lurks,a Beau Brummell sticking in its three-

cornered always moist mouth)—jazz,
for whose twitching lips,between you and me
almost succeeds while toddle rings the bell.
But if her tall corpsecoloured body seat
itself(with the uncouth habitual dull
jerk at garters)there's no sharpest neat
word for the thing.
              Her voice?
                           gruesome:a trull
leaps from the lungs "gimme uh swell fite

like up ter yknow,Rektuz,Toysday nite;
where uh guy gets gayn troze uh lobstersalad

## IV. MARJ

"life?

       Listen" the feline she with radishred
legs said(crossing them slowly)"I'm
asleep.  Yep.  Youse is asleep kid
and everybody is."  And i hazarded
"god"(blushing slightly)—"O damn
ginks like dis Gawd" opening slowlyslowly
them—then carefully the rolypoly
voice squatting on a mountain of gum did
something like a whisper,"even her."
"The Madam?" I emitted;vaguely watching
that mountainous worthy in the fragile act
of doing her eyebrows.—Marj's laughter smacked
me:pummeling the curtains,drooped to a purr...

i left her permanently smiling

## V. FRAN

should i entirely ask of god why
on the alert neck of this brittle whore
delicately wobbles an improbably distinct face,
and how these wooden big two feet conclude
happeningly the unfirm drooping bloated
calves
                i would receive the answer more
or less deserved,Young fellow go in peace.
which i do,being as Dick Mid once noted
lifting a Green River(here's to youse)
"a bloke wot's well behaved"...and always try
to not wonder how let's say elation
causes the bent eyes thickly to protrude—

or why her tiniest whispered invitation
is like a clock striking in a dark house

POEM, OR BEAUTY HURTS MR. VINAL

take it from me kiddo
believe me
my country,'tis of

you,land of the Cluett
Shirt Boston Garter and Spearmint
Girl With The Wrigley Eyes(of you
land of the Arrow Ide
and Earl &
Wilson
Collars)of you i
sing:land of Abraham Lincoln and Lydia E. Pinkham,
land above all of Just Add Hot Water And Serve—
from every B.V.D.

let freedom ring

amen.  i do however protest,anent the un
-spontaneous and otherwise scented merde which
greets one(Everywhere Why)as divine poesy per
that and this radically defunct periodical.  i would

suggest that certain ideas gestures
rhymes,like Gillette Razor Blades
having been used and reused
to the mystical moment of dullness emphatically are
Not To Be Resharpened.  (Case in point

if we are to believe these gently O sweetly
melancholy trillers amid the thrillers
these crepuscular violinists among my and your
skyscrapers—Helen & Cleopatra were Just Too Lovely,
The Snail's On The Thorn enter Morn and God's
In His andsoforth

do you get me?)according
to such supposedly indigenous
throstles Art is O World O Life
a formula:example,Turn Your Shirttails Into
Drawers and If It Isn't An Eastman It Isn't A
Kodak therefore my friends let
us now sing each and all fortissimo A-
mer
i

ca, I
love,
You.  And there're a
hun-dred-mil-lion-oth-ers,like
all of you successfully if
delicately gelded(or spaded)
gentlemen(and ladies)—pretty

littleliverpill-
hearted-Nujolneeding-There's-A-Reason
americans(who tensetendoned and with
upward vacant eyes,painfully
perpetually crouched,quivering,upon the
sternly allotted sandpile
—how silently
emit a tiny violetflavoured nuisance:Odor?

ono.
comes out like a ribbon lies flat on the brush

nobody loses all the time

i had an uncle named
Sol who was a born failure and
nearly everybody said he should have gone
into vaudeville perhaps because my Uncle Sol could
sing McCann He Was A Diver on Xmas Eve like Hell Itself which
may or may not account for the fact that my Uncle

Sol indulged in that possibly most inexcusable
of all to use a highfalootin phrase
luxuries that is or to
wit farming and be
it needlessly
added

my Uncle Sol's farm
failed because the chickens
ate the vegetables so
my Uncle Sol had a
chicken farm till the
skunks ate the chickens when

my Uncle Sol
had a skunk farm but
the skunks caught cold and
died and so
my Uncle Sol imitated the
skunks in a subtle manner

or by drowning himself in the watertank
but somebody who'd given my Uncle Sol a Victor
Victrola and records while he lived presented to
him upon the auspicious occasion of his decease a
scrumptious not to mention splendiferous funeral with
tall boys in black gloves and flowers and everything and

i remember we all cried like the Missouri
when my Uncle Sol's coffin lurched because
somebody pressed a button
(and down went
my Uncle
Sol

and started a worm farm)

# 125

(and i imagine
never mind Joe agreeably cheerfully remarked when
surrounded by fat stupid animals
the jewess shrieked
the messiah tumbled successfully into the world
the animals continued eating.   And i imagine she,and
heard them slobber and
in the darkness)

stood sharp angels with faces like Jim Europe

curtains part)
the peacockappareled
prodigy of Flo's midnight
Frolic dolores

small in the head keen chassied like a Rolls
Royce
swoops smoothly
                        outward(amid
tinkling-cheering-hammering

tables)

while softly along Kirkland Street
the infantile ghost of Professor
Royce rolls

remembering that it

has for
-gotten some-
thing ah

(my

necktie

Jimmie's got a goil
                goil
                      goil,
                            Jimmie
's got a goil and
she coitnly can shimmie

when you see her shake
                      shake
                            shake,
                                  when
you see her shake a
shimmie how you wish that you was Jimmie.

Oh for such a gurl
                  gurl
                      gurl,
                            oh
for such a gurl to
be a fellow's twistandtwirl

talk about your Sal-
                    Sal-
                        Sal-,
                              talk
about your Salo
-mes but gimmie Jimmie's gal.

listen my children and you
shall hear the true

story of Mr Do
-nothing the wellknown parvenu
who

(having dreamed of a corkscrew)
studied with Freud a year or two
and when Freud got through
with Do-

nothing Do
-nothing could do
nothing which you
and i are accustomed to
accomplish two

or three times,and even a few
more depending on the remu-
nerativeness of the stimulus(eheu
fu
-gaces Postu-
me boo

who)

# 129

this man is o so
Waiter
this;woman is

please shut that
the pout And affectionate leer
interminable pyramidal,napkins
(this man is oh so tired of this
a door opens by itself
woman.)they so to speak were in

Love once?
now
        her mouth opens too far
and:she attacks her Lobster without
feet mingle under the
mercy.
                (exit the hors d'œuvres)

# 130

---

yonder deadfromtheneckup graduate of a
somewhat obscure to be sure university spends
her time looking picturesque under

the as it happens quite
erroneous impression that he

nascitur

# 131

?

why are these pipples taking their hets off?
the king & queen
alighting from their limousine
inhabit the Hôtel Meurice(whereas
i live in a garret and eat aspirine)

but who is this pale softish almost round
young man to whom headwaiters bow so?
hush—the author of Women By Night whose latest Seeds
Of Evil sold 69 carloads before
publication the girl who goes wrong you

know(whereas when i lie down i cough too
much). How did the traffic get so jammed?
bedad it is the famous doctor who inserts
monkeyglands in millionaires a cute idea n'est-ce pas?
(whereas,upon the other hand,myself)but let us next demand

wherefore yon mob
an accident?somebody got concus-
sion of the brain?—Not
a bit of it,my dears merely the prime
minister of Siam in native

costume,who
emerging from a pissoir
enters abruptly Notre Dame(whereas
de gustibus non disputandum est
my lady is tired of That sort of thing

this young question mark man

question mark
who suffers from
indigestion question
mark is a remarkably
charming person

personally they tell

me as for me
i only knows that
as far as
his pictures goes

he's a wet dream

by Cézanne

mr youse needn't be so spry
concernin questions arty

each has his tastes but as for i
i likes a certain party

gimme the he-man's solid bliss
for youse ideas i'll match youse

a pretty girl who naked is
is worth a million statues

# 134

she being Brand

-new;and you
know consequently a
little stiff i was
careful of her and(having

thoroughly oiled the universal
joint tested my gas felt of
her radiator made sure her springs were O.

K.)i went right to it flooded-the-carburetor cranked her

up,slipped the
clutch(and then somehow got into reverse she
kicked what
the hell)next
minute i was back in neutral tried and

again slo-wly;bare,ly nudg.   ing(my

lev-er Right-
oh and her gears being in
A 1 shape passed
from low through
second-in-to-high like
greased lightning just as we turned the corner of Divinity

avenue i touched the accelerator and give

her the juice,good

(it

was the first ride and believe i we was
happy to see how nice she acted right up to
the last minute coming back down by the Public
Gardens i slammed on

the
internalexpanding
&
externalcontracting
brakes Bothatonce and

brought allofher tremB
-ling
to a:dead.

stand-
;Still)

# 135

IKEY(GOLDBERG)'S WORTH I'M
TOLD $ SEVERAL MILLION
FINKLESTEIN(FRITZ)LIVES
AT THE RITZ WEAR
earl & wilson COLLARS

# 136

oDE

o

the sweet & aged people
who rule this world(and me and
you if we're not very
careful)

O,

the darling benevolent mindless
He—and She—
shaped waxworks filled
with dead ideas(the oh

quintillions of incredible
dodderingly godly toothless
always-so-much-interested-
in-everybody-else's-business

bipeds)OH
the bothering
dear unnecessary hairless
o

ld

# 137

on the Madam's best april the
twenty nellie

anyway and
it's flutters everything
queer;does smells he smiles is
like Out of doors he's a with
eyes and making twice the a week
you kind of,know(kind well of
A sort of the way he smile but
and her a I mean me a
Irish,cook but well oh don't
you makes burst want to dear somehow
quickyes when(now,dark dear oh)
the iceman
how,luminously
oh how listens and,expands
my somewherealloverme heart my
the halfgloom coolish
of The what are
parks for wiggle yes has
are leap,which,anyway

give rapid lapfuls of
idiotic big hands

# 138

stop look &

listen Venezia:incline thine
ear you glassworks
of Murano;
pause
elevator nel
mezzo del cammin' that means half-
way up the Campanile,believe

thou me cocodrillo—

mine eyes have seen
the glory of

the coming of
the Americans particularly the
brand of marriageable nymph which is
armed with large legs rancid
voices Baedekers Mothers and kodaks
—by night upon the Riva Schiavoni or in
the felicitous vicinity of the de l'Europe

Grand and Royal
Danielli their numbers

are like unto the stars of Heaven....

i do signore
affirm that all gondola signore
day below me gondola signore gondola
and above me pass loudly and gondola
rapidly denizens of Omaha Altoona or what
not enthusiastic cohorts from Duluth God only,
gondola knows Cincingondolanati i gondola don't

—the substantial dollarbringing virgins

"from the Loggia where
are we angels by O yes
beautiful we now pass through the look
girls in the style of that's the
foliage what is it didn't Ruskin
says about you got the haven't Marjorie
isn't this wellcurb simply darling"
                                        —O Education:O
thos cook & son

(O to be a metope
now that triglyph's here)

(as that named Fred
-someBody:hippopotamus,scratch-
ing,one,knee with,its,
friend observes I

pass Mr Tom Larsen twirls among

pale lips the extinct
cigar)at

which

this(once flinger
of lariats lean exroper of
horned suddenly crashing things)man spits

quickly into the very bright spittoon

my uncle
Daniel fought in the civil
war band and can play the triangle
like the devil)my

uncle Frank has done nothing for many
years but fly kites and
when the
string breaks(or something)my uncle Frank breaks into
tears.   my uncle Tom

knits and is a kewpie above the ears(but

my uncle Ed
that's
dead from the neck

up is led all over
Brattle Street by a castrated pup

# 141

---

poets yeggs and thirsties

since we are spanked and put to sleep by dolls let
us not be continually astonished should
from their actions and speeches
sawdust perpetually leak

rather is it between such beddings and
bumpings of ourselves to be observed
how in this fundamental respect the well
recognised regime of childhood is reversed

meantime in dreams let us investigate
thoroughly each one his optima rerum first
having taken care to lie upon our
abdomens for greater privacy and lest

punished bottoms interrupt philosophy

# 142

---

a man who had fallen among thieves
lay by the roadside on his back
dressed in fifteenthrate ideas
wearing a round jeer for a hat

fate per a somewhat more than less
emancipated evening
had in return for consciousness
endowed him with a changeless grin

whereon a dozen staunch and leal
citizens did graze at pause
then fired by hypercivic zeal
sought newer pastures or because

swaddled with a frozen brook
of pinkest vomit out of eyes
which noticed nobody he looked
as if he did not care to rise

one hand did nothing on the vest
its wideflung friend clenched weakly dirt
while the mute trouserfly confessed
a button solemnly inert.

Brushing from whom the stiffened puke
i put him all into my arms
and staggered banged with terror through
a million billion trillion stars

opening of the chambers close

quotes the microscopic pithecoid President
in a new frock
coat(scrambling all
up over the tribune dances crazily
& &)&
chatters about Peacepeacepeace(to
droppingly
descend amid thunderous anthropoid applause)pronounced

by the way Pay the

extremely artistic nevertobeextinguished fla
-me of the(very prettily indeed)arra-
nged souvenir of the in spite of himself fa
-mous soldier minus his na-
me(so as not to hurt the perspective of the(hei
-nous thought)otherwise immaculately tabulated vicinity)invei-
gles a few mildly curious rai
-ned on people(both male and female
created He

then,     And every beast of the field

# 144

the season 'tis,my lovely lambs,

of Summer Volstead Christ and Co.
the epoch of Mann's righteousness
the age of dollars and no sense.
Which being quite beyond dispute

as prove from Troy(N.Y.)to Cairo
(Egypt)the luminous dithyrambs
of large immaculate unmute
antibolshevistic gents
(each manufacturing word by word
his own unrivalled brand of pyro
-technic blurb anent the(hic)
hero dead that gladly(sic)
in far lands perished of unheard
of maladies including flu)

my little darlings,let us now
passionately remember how—
braving the worst,of peril heedless,
each braver than the other,each
(a typewriter within his reach)
upon his fearless derrière
sturdily seated—Colonel Needless
To Name and General You know who
a string of pretty medals drew

(while messrs jack james john and jim
in token of their country's love
received my dears the order of
The Artificial Arm and Limb)

—or,since bloodshed and kindred questions
inhibit unprepared digestions,
come:let us mildly contemplate
beginning with his wellfilled pants
earth's biggest grafter,nothing less;
the Honorable Mr.(guess)
who,breathing on the ear of fate,
landed a seat in the legislat-
ure whereas tommy so and so
(an erring child of circumstance
whom the bulls nabbed at 33rd)

pulled six months for selling snow

life hurl my
yes,crumbles hand(ful released conarefetti)ev eryflitter,inga. where
mil(lions of aflickf)litter ing brightmillion ofS hurl;edindodg:ing
whom areEyes shy-dodge is bright cruMbshandful,quick-hurl edinwho
Is flittercrumbs,fluttercrimbs are floatfallin,g:allwhere:
a:crimbflitteringish is arefloatsis ingfallall!mil,shy milbrightlions
my(hurl flicker handful
in)dodging are shybrigHteyes is crum bs(alll)if,ey Es

# 146

16 heures
l'Etoile

the communists have fine Eyes

some are young some old none
look alike the flics rush
batter the crowd sprawls collapses
singing knocked down trampled the kicked by
flics rush(the

Flics,tidiyum,are
very tidiyum reassuringly similar,
they all have very tidiyum
mustaches,and very
tidiyum chins,and just above
their very tidiyum ears their
very tidiyum necks begin)
                              let us add

that there are 50(fifty)flics for every
one(1)communist and
all the flics are very organically
arranged
and their nucleus(composed
of captains in freshly-creased
-uniforms with only-just-
shined buttons
tidiyum
before and behind)has a nucleolus:

the Prefect of Police

(a dapper derbied
creature,swaggers daintily
twiddling
his tiny cane
and,mazurkas about tweak-
ing his wing collar pecking at his im

-peccable cravat directing being
shooting his cuffs
saluted everywhere saluting
reviewing processions of minions
tappingpeopleontheback

"allezcirculez")

—my    he's brave....
the
communists pick
up themselves friends
& their hats legs &

arms brush dirt coats
smile looking hands
spit blood teeth

the Communists have(very)fine eyes

(which stroll hither and thither through the
evening in bruised narrow questioning faces)

# 147

---

"next to of course god america i
love you land of the pilgrims' and so forth oh
say can you see by the dawn's early my
country 'tis of centuries come and go
and are no more what of it we should worry
in every language even deafanddumb
thy sons acclaim your glorious name by gorry
by jingo by gee by gosh by gum
why talk of beauty what could be more beautiful than these heroic happy dead
who rushed like lions to the roaring slaughter
they did not stop to think they died instead
then shall the voice of liberty be mute?"

He spoke.  And drank rapidly a glass of water

# 148

my sweet old etcetera
aunt lucy during the recent

war could and what
is more did tell you just
what everybody was fighting

for,
my sister

isabel created hundreds
(and
hundreds)of socks not to
mention shirts fleaproof earwarmers

etcetera wristers etcetera,my
mother hoped that

i would die etcetera
bravely of course my father used
to become hoarse talking about how it was
a privilege and if only he
could meanwhile my

self etcetera lay quietly
in the deep mud et

cetera
(dreaming,
et
  cetera,of
Your smile
eyes knees and of your Etcetera)

# 149

come,gaze with me upon this dome
of many coloured glass,and see
his mother's pride,his father's joy,
unto whom duty whispers low

"thou must!" and who replies "I can!"
—yon clean upstanding well dressed boy
that with his peers full oft hath quaffed
the wine of life and found it sweet—

a tear within his stern blue eye,
upon his firm white lips a smile,
one thought alone:to do or die
for God for country and for Yale

above his blond determined head
the sacred flag of truth unfurled,
in the bright heyday of his youth
the upper class American

unsullied stands,before the world:
with manly heart and conscience free,
upon the front steps of her home
by the high minded pure young girl

much kissed,by loving relatives
well fed,and fully photographed
the son of man goes forth to war
with trumpets clap and syphilis

# 150
---

it's jolly
odd what pops into
your jolly tête when the
jolly shells begin dropping jolly fast you
hear the rrmp and
then nearerandnearerandNEARER
and before
you can

!

& we're

NOT
(oh—
—i say

that's jolly odd
old thing,jolly
odd,jolly
jolly odd isn't
it jolly odd.

# 151

lis
-ten

you know what i mean when
the first guy drops you know
everybody feels sick or
when they throw in a few gas
and the oh baby shrapnel
or my feet getting dim freezing or
up to your you know what in water or
with the bugs crawling right all up
all everywhere over you all me everyone
that's been there knows what
i mean a god damned lot of
people don't and never
never
will know,
they don't want

to
no

# 152

look at this)
a 75 done
this nobody would
have believed
would they no
kidding this was my particular

pal
funny aint
it we was
buddies
i used to

know
him lift the
poor cuss
tenderly this side up handle

with care
fragile
and send him home

to his old mother in
a new nice pine box

(collect

than(by yon sunset's wintry glow
revealed)this tall strong stalwart youth,
what sight shall human optics know
more quite ennobling forsooth?

One wondrous fine sonofabitch
(to all purposes and intents)
in which distinct and rich
portrait should be included,gents

these(by the fire's ruddy glow
united)not less than sixteen
children and of course you know
their mother,of his heart the queen

—incalculable bliss!
Picture it gents:our hero,Dan
who as you've guessed already is
the poorbuthonest workingman

(by that bright flame whose myriad tints
enrich a visage simple,terse,
seated like any king or prince
upon his uncorrupted arse

with all his hearty soul aglow)
his nightly supper sups
it isn't snowing snow you know
it's snowing buttercups

# 154

but if i should say
goodmorning trouble adds
up all sorts of quickly
things on the slate of that
nigger's
face(but

If i should say thankyouverymuch

mr rosenbloom picks strawberries
with beringed hands)but if

i Should say solong my
tailor
chuckles

like a woman in a dream(but if i
should say
Now the all saucers
but cups if begin to spoons dance every-

should where say over the damned table and we
hold lips Eyes everything
hands you know what
happens)but if i should,
Say,

Will i ever forget that precarious moment?

As i was standing on the third rail waiting for the next train to grind me into lifeless atoms various absurd thoughts slyly crept into my highly sexed mind.

It seemed to me that i had first of all really made quite a mistake in being at all born,seeing that i was wifeless and only half awake,cursed with pimples,correctly dressed,cleanshaven above the nombril,and much to my astonishment much impressed by having once noticed (as an infantile phenomenon)George Washington almost incompletely surrounded by welldrawn icecakes beheld being too strong,in brief:an American,if you understand that i mean what i say i believe my most intimate friends would never have gathered.

A collarbutton which had always not nothurt me not much and in the same place.

Why according to tomorrow's paper the proletariat will not rise yesterday.

Inexpressible itchings to be photographed with Lord Rothermere playing with Lord Rothermere billiards very well by moonlight with Lord Rothermere.

A crocodile eats a native,who in revenge beats it insensible with a banana,establishing meanwhile a religious cult based on consubstantial intangibility.

Personne ne m'aime et j'ai les mains froides.

His Royal Highness said "peek-a-boo" and thirty tame fleas left the prettily embroidered howdah immediately.

Thumbprints of an angel named Frederick found on a lightningrod,Boston,Mass.

such were the not unhurried reflections to which my organ of imperception gave birth to which i should ordinarily have objected to which,considering the background,it is hardly surprising if anyone hardly should call exactly extraordinary. We refer,of course,to my position. A bachelor incapable of occupation,he had long suppressed the desire to suppress the suppressed desire of shall we say:Idleness,while meaning its opposite? Nothing could be clearer to all concerned than that i am not a policeman.

Meanwhile the tea regressed.

Kipling again H. G. Wells,and Anatole France shook hands again and yet again shook again hands again,the former coachman with a pipewrench of the again latter then opening a box of newly without exaggeration shot with some difficulty sardines. Mr. Wiggin took Wrs. Miggin's harm in is,extinguishing the spittoon by a candle furnished by courtesy of the management on Thursdays,opposite which a church stood perfectly upright but not piano item:a watermelon causes indigestion to William Cullen Longfellow's small negro son,Henry Wadsworth Bryant.

By this time,however,the flight of crows had ceased. I withdrew my hands from the tennisracket. All was over. One brief convulsive octopus,and then our hero folded his umbrella.

It seemed too beautiful.

Let us perhaps excuse me if i repeat himself:these,or nearly these,were the not unpainful thoughts which occupied the subject of our attention;to speak even less objectively,i was horribly scared i would actually fall off the rail before the really train after all arrived.  If i should have made this perfectly clear,it entirely would have been not my fault.

# 156

candles and

Here Comes a glass box
which the exhumed
hand of Saint Ignatz miraculously
inhabits. (people tumble
down. people crumble to their
knees. people
begin crossing people)and

hErE cOmEs a glass box:
surrounded by priests
moving in fifty colours
,sensuously

(the crowd
howls faintly
blubbering pointing

see
yes)
It
here
comes

A Glass
Box and incense with

and oh sunlight—
the crash of the
colours(of the oh
silently
striding)priests-and-
slowly,al,ways;procession:and

Enters

this
      church.

toward which The
Expectant stutter(upon artificial limbs,
with faces like defunct geraniums)

# 157

---

voices to voices,lip to lip
i swear(to noone everyone)constitutes
undying;or whatever this and that petal confutes...
to exist being a peculiar form of sleep

what's beyond logic happens beneath will;
nor can these moments be translated:i say
that even after April
by God there is no excuse for May

—bring forth your flowers and machinery:sculpture and prose
flowers guess and miss
machinery is the more accurate,yes
it delivers the goods,Heaven knows

(yet are we mindful,though not as yet awake,
of ourselves which shout and cling,being
for a little while and which easily break
in spite of the best overseeing)

i mean that the blond absence of any program
except last and always and first to live
makes unimportant what i and you believe;
not for philosophy does this rose give a damn...

bring on your fireworks,which are a mixed
splendor of piston and of pistil;very well
provided an instant may be fixed
so that it will not rub,like any other pastel.

(While you and i have lips and voices which
are for kissing and to sing with
who cares if some oneeyed son of a bitch
invents an instrument to measure Spring with?

each dream nascitur,is not made...)
why then to Hell with that:the other;this,
since the thing perhaps is
to eat flowers and not to be afraid.

# 158

weazened Irrefutable unastonished
two,countenances seated in arranging;sunlight
with-ered unspea-king:tWeNtY,f i n g e r s,large
four gnarled lips totter

Therefore,approaching my twentysix selves
bulging in immortal Spring express a cry of
How do you find the sun,ladies?

(graduallyverygradually "there is not enough
of it" their,hands
minutely

answered

# 159

it really must
be Nice,never to

have no imagination)or never
never to wonder about guys you used to(and them
slim hot queens with dam next to nothing

on)tangoing
(while a feller tries
to hold down the fifty bucks per
job with one foot and rock a

cradle with the other)it Must be
nice never to have no doubts about why you
put the ring
on(and watching her
face grow old and tired to which

you're married and hands get red washing
things and dishes)and to never,never really wonder i
mean about the smell
of babies and how you

know the dam rent's going to and everything and never,never
Never to stand at no window
because i can't sleep(smoking sawdust

cigarettes in the
middle of the night

# 160

---

death is more than
certain a hundred these
sounds crowds odours it
is in a hurry
beyond that any this
taxi smile or angle we do

not sell and buy
things so necessary as
is death and unlike shirts
neckties trousers
we cannot wear it out

no sir which is why
granted who discovered
America ether the movies
may claim general importance

to me to you nothing is
what particularly
matters hence in a

little sunlight and less
moonlight ourselves against the worms

hate laugh shimmy

now that fierce few
flowers(stealthily)
in the alive west
begin

requiescat this six
feet of Breton big good
body,which terminated
in fists hair wood

erect cursing hatless who
(bent by wind)slammed hard-
over the tiller;clattered
forward skidding in outrageous

sabots language trickling
pried his black
mouth with fat jibing
lips,

once upon a
(that is
over:and the sea heaving
indolent colourless forgets)time

Requiescat.
carry
carefully the blessed large silent him
into nibbling final worms

Among
      these
           red pieces of
day(against which and
quite silently hills
made of blueandgreen paper

scorchbend ingthem
-selves-U
pcurv E,into:
           anguish(clim
b)ing
s-p-i-r-a-
l
 and,disappear)
           Satanic and blasé

a black goat lookingly wanders

There is nothing left of the world but
into this noth
ing il treno per
Roma si-gnori?
jerk.
ilyr,ushes

it is winter a moon in the afternoon
and warm air turning into January darkness up
through which sprouting gently,the cathedral
leans its dreamy spine against thick sunset

i perceive in front of our lady a ring of people
a brittle swoon of centrifugally expecting
faces clumsily which devours a man,three cats,
five white mice,and a baboon.

O a monkey with a sharp face waddling carefully
the length of this padded pole;a monkey attached
by a chain securely to this always talking
individual,mysterious witty hatless.

Cats which move smoothly from neck to neck of bottles,cats
smoothly willowing out and in between bottles,who step
        smoothly
and rapidly along this pole over five squirming
mice;or leap through hoops of fire,creating smoothness.

People stare,the drunker applaud
while twilight takes the sting out of the vermilion
jacket of nodding hairy Jaqueline who is given a mouse
to hold lovingly,

our lady what do you think of this?   Do your proud
        fingers and
your arms tremble remembering something squirming fragile
and which had been presented unto you by a mystery?
...the cathedral recedes into weather without answering

# 164

will out of the kindness of their hearts a few philosophers tell me
what am i doing on top of this hill at Calchidas,in the sunlight?
down ever so far on the beach below me a little girl in white spins,
    tumbles;rolling in sand.
across this water,crowding tints:browns and whites shoving,the
    dotting millions of windows of thousands of houses—
    Lisboa.   Like the crackle of a typewriter,in the afternoon sky.
goats and sheep are driven by somebody along a curve of road
    which eats into a pink cliff back and up leaning out of
    yellowgreen water.

they are building a house down there by the sea,in the afternoon.

rapidly a reddish ant travels my fifth finger.
a bird chirps in a tree,somewhere nowhere
and a little girl in white is tumbling
in sand
        Clouds over
me are like bridegrooms

Naked and luminous

                (here  the  absurd  I;life,to  peer  and  wear
                clothes.   i am altogether foolish,i sud-
                denly make a fist out of ten fingers
voices rise from down ever so far—
hush.
        Sunlight,
                there are old men behind me I tell you;several,
                incredible,sleepy

# 165

(ponder,darling,these busted statues
of yon motheaten forum be aware
notice what hath remained
—the stone cringes
clinging to the stone,how obsolete

lips utter their extant smile....
remark

a few deleted of texture
or meaning monuments and dolls

resist Them Greediest Paws of careful
time all of which is extremely
unimportant)whereas Life

matters if or

when the your- and my-
idle vertical worthless
self unite in a peculiarly
momentary

partnership(to instigate
constructive
                    Horizontal
business....even so,let us make haste
—consider well this ruined aqueduct

lady,
which used to lead something into somewhere)

# 166

here's a little mouse)and
what does he think about,i
wonder as over this
floor(quietly with

bright eyes)drifts(nobody
can tell because
Nobody knows,or why
jerks Here &,here,
gr(oo)ving the room's Silence)this like
a littlest
poem a
(with wee ears and see?

tail frisks)
                    (gonE)
"mouse",
              We are not the same you and

i,since here's a little he
or is
it It
?    (or was something we saw in the mirror)?

therefore we'll kiss;for maybe
what was Disappeared
into ourselves
who     (look).        ,startled

but observe;although
once is never the beginning of
enough,is it(i do not pretend
to know the reason any more than.)   But look:up-

raising,hoisting,a little
perhaps that and this,deftly
propping on smallest hands
the slim hinging you
                              —because
it's five o'clock

and these(i notice)trees winterbrief surly old
gurgle a nonsense of sparrows,the cathedral
shudders blackening;
the sky is washed with tone

now for a moon
to squat in first darkness
—a little moon thinner than

memory

faint
-er
      than all the whys
which lurk
between your naked shoulderblades.—Here
comes a stout fellow in a blouse
just outside this window,touching the glass
boxes one by one with his magic
stick(in which a willing
bulb of flame bubbles)
                              see

here and here they explode
silently into crocuses of brightness.   (That is enough
of life,for you.   I understand.   Once
again....)sliding

a little downward,embrace me with your body's suddenly
curving entire warm questions

in spite of everything
which breathes and moves,since Doom
(with white longest hands
neatening each crease)
will smooth entirely our minds

—before leaving my room
i turn,and(stooping
through the morning)kiss
this pillow,dear
where our heads lived and were.

# 169

it is so long since my heart has been with yours

shut by our mingling arms through
a darkness where new lights begin and
increase,
since your mind has walked into
my kiss as a stranger
into the streets and colours of a town—

that i have perhaps forgotten
how,always(from
these hurrying crudities
of blood and flesh)Love
coins His most gradual gesture,

and whittles life to eternity

—after which our separating selves become museums
filled with skilfully stuffed memories

# 170

---

supposing i dreamed this)
only imagine,when day has thrilled
you are a house around which
i am a wind—

your walls will not reckon how
strangely my life is curved
since the best he can do
is to peer through windows,unobserved

—listen,for(out of all
things)dream is noone's fool;
if this wind who i am prowls
carefully around this house of you

love being such,or such,
the normal corners of your heart
will never guess how much
my wonderful jealousy is dark

if light should flower:
or laughing sparkle from
the shut house(around and around
which a poor wind will roam

# 171

i am a beggar always
who begs in your mind

(slightly smiling,patient,unspeaking
with a sign on his
breast
BLIND)yes i

am this person of whom somehow
you are never wholly rid(and who

does not ask for more than
just enough dreams to
live on)
        after all,kid

you might as well
toss him a few thoughts

a little love preferably,
anything which you can't
pass off on other people:for
instance a
plugged promise—

then he will maybe(hearing something
fall into his hat)go wandering
after it with fingers;till having

found
what was thrown away
        himself
taptaptaps out of your brain,hopes,life

to(carefully turning a
corner)never bother you any more.

# 172

if within tonight's erect
everywhere of black muscles fools
a weightless slowness(deftly

muting the world's texture with drifted

gifts of featheriest slenderness and
how gradually which descending are suddenly
received)or by doomful connivance

accurately thither and hither myself

struts unremembered(rememberingly
with in both pockets curled hands moves)
why then toward morning he is a ghost whom

assault these whispering fists of hail

(and a few windows awaken certain faces
busily horribly blunder through new light
hush we are made of the same thing as perhaps

nothing,he murmurs carefully lying down)

# 173

i go to this window

just as day dissolves
when it is twilight(and
looking up in fear

i see the new moon
thinner than a hair)

making me feel
how myself has been coarse and dull
compared with you,silently who are
and cling
to my mind always

But now she sharpens and becomes crisper
until i smile with knowing
—and all about
herself

the sprouting largest final air

plunges
            inward with hurled
downward thousands of enormous dreams

# 174

you are not going to,dear.   You are not going to and
i but that doesn't in the least matter.   The big
fear Who held us deeply in His fist is

no longer,can you imagine it
i can't which doesn't matter
and what does is possibly this dear,that we may resume
impact with the inutile collide

once more with the imaginable,love,and eat sunlight(do
you believe it?   i begin to and that doesn't matter)which

i suggest teach us a new terror always
which shall brighten
carefully these things we consider life.
Dear i put my eyes into you but that doesn't matter
further than of old

because you fooled the doctors,i touch you with hopes and
words and with so and so:we are together,we will
kiss or smile or move.   It's different too isn't it

different dear from moving as we,you
and i,used to move when i thought you were going to(but
that doesn't matter)
when you thought you were going to America.
                                        Then


moving was a matter of not keeping still;we were
two alert lice in the blond hair of nothing

# 175

if being mortised with a dream
myself speaks

(whispering,
suggesting that our souls
inhabit whatever is between them)
knowing my lips hands the way i move
my habits laughter

i say
you will perhaps pardon,
possibly you will comprehend.   and how
this has arrived your mind may guess

if at sunset
it should,leaning against me,smile;
or(between dawn and twilight)giving

your eyes,present me also
with the terror of shrines

which noone has suspected(but
wherein silently
always
are kneeling the various deaths
which are your lover lady:together with what keen
innumerable lives he has not lived.

sunlight was over
our mouths fears hearts lungs arms hopes feet hands

under us the unspeaking Mediterranean bluer
than we had imagined
a few cries drifting through
high air
a sail a fishing boat somebody an invisible spectator,
maybe certain nobodies laughing faintly

playing moving far below us

perhaps one villa caught like pieces
of a kite in the trees,here
and here reflecting
sunlight
(everywhere sunlight keen complete
silent

and everywhere you your kisses your flesh mind breathing
beside under around myself)
                              by and by

a fat colour reared itself against the sky and the sea

...finally your eyes knew
me,we smiled to each other,releasing lay,watching
(sprawling,in
grass upon a
cliff)what had been something
else carefully slowly fatally turning into ourselves...

while in the very middle of fire all

the world becoming bright and little melted.

# 177

how this uncouth enchanted
person,arising from a
restaurant,looks breathes or moves
—climbing(past light after
light)to turn,disappears

the very swift and
invisibly living
rhythm of your Heart possibly

will understand;
or why(in

this most exquisite of cities)all
of the long night a fragile imitation of
(perhaps)myself carefully wanders
streets dark and,deep

with rain....

(he,slightly whom or
cautiously this person

and this imitation resemble,
descends into the earth with the year
a cigarette between his ghost-lips

gradually)
remembering badly,softly
your
kissed thrice suddenly smile

# 178

the moon looked into my window
it touched me with its small hands
and with curling infantile
fingers it understood my eyes cheeks mouth
its hands(slipping)felt of my necktie wandered
against my shirt and into my body the
sharp things fingered tinily my heart life

the little hands withdrew,jerkily,themselves

quietly they began playing with a button
the moon smiled she
let go my vest and crept
through the window
she did not fall
she went creeping along the air
                              over houses
                                    roofs

And out of the east toward
her a fragile light bent gatheringly

# 179

you are like the snow only
purer fleeter,like the rain
only sweeter frailer you

whom certain
flowers resemble but trembling(cowards
which fear
to miss within your least gesture the hurting
skill which lives)and since

nothing lingers
beyond a little instant,
along with rhyme and with laughter
O my lady
(and every brittle marvelous breathing thing)

since i and you are on our ways to dust

of your fragility
(but chiefly of your smile,
most suddenly which is
of love and death a marriage)you give me

courage
so that against myself
the sharp days slobber in vain:

Nor am i afraid that
this,which we call autumn,cleverly
dies and over the ripe world wanders with
a near and careful
smile in his mouth(making

everything suddenly old and with his awkward eyes
pushing
sleep under and thoroughly
into all beautiful things)

winter,whom Spring shall kill

# 180

since feeling is first
who pays any attention
to the syntax of things
will never wholly kiss you;

wholly to be a fool
while Spring is in the world

my blood approves,
and kisses are a better fate
than wisdom
lady i swear by all flowers.  Don't cry
—the best gesture of my brain is less than
your eyelids' flutter which says

we are for each other:then
laugh,leaning back in my arms
for life's not a paragraph

And death i think is no parenthesis

our touching hearts slenderly comprehend
(clinging as fingers,loving one another
gradually into hands)and bend
into the huge disaster of the year:

like this most early single star which tugs

weakly at twilight,caught in thickening fear
our slightly fingering spirits starve and smother;
until autumn abruptly wholly hugs

our dying silent minds,which hand in hand
at some window try to understand
the
   (through pale miles of perishing air,haunted
with huddling infinite wishless melancholy,
suddenly looming)accurate undaunted

moon's bright third tumbling slowly

# 182

because
you go away i give roses who
will advise even yourself,lady
in the most certainly(of what we
everywhere do not touch)deep
things;
         remembering ever so
tinily these,your crisp
eyes actually shall contain new faeries

(and if your slim lips are amused,no wisest

painter of fragile
Marys will understand
how smiling may be made as
skilfully.)   But carry
also,with that indolent and with
this flower wholly whom you do
not ever fear,
                  me in your heart

softly;not all
but the beginning

of mySelf

you being in love
will tell who softly asks in love,

am i separated from your body smile brain hands merely
to become the jumping puppets of a dream?   oh i mean:
entirely having in my careful how
careful arms created this at length
inexcusable,this inexplicable pleasure—you go from several
persons:believe me that strangers arrive
when i have kissed you into a memory
slowly,oh seriously
—that since and if you disappear

solemnly
myselves
ask "life,the question how do i drink dream smile

and how do i prefer this face to another and
why do i weep eat sleep—what does the whole intend"
they wonder.oh and they cry "to be,being,that i am alive
this absurd fraction in its lowest terms
with everything cancelled
but shadows
—what does it all come down to?  love?  Love
if you like and i like,for the reason that i
hate people and lean out of this window is love,love
and the reason that i laugh and breathe is oh love and the reason

that i do not fall into this street is love."

along the brittle treacherous bright streets
of memory comes my heart,singing like
an idiot,whispering like a drunken man

who(at a certain corner,suddenly)meets
the tall policeman of my mind.
                              awake
being not asleep,elsewhere our dreams began
which now are folded:but the year completes
his life as a forgotten prisoner

—"Ici?"—"Ah non,mon chéri;il fait trop froid"—
they are gone:along these gardens moves a wind bringing
rain and leaves,filling the air with fear
and sweetness....pauses.   (Halfwhispering....halfsinging

stirs the always smiling chevaux de bois)

when you were in Paris we met here

some ask praise of their fellows
but i being otherwise
made compose curves
and yellows,angles or silences
to a less erring end)

myself is sculptor of
your body's idiom:
the musician of your wrists;
the poet who is afraid
only to mistranslate

a rhythm in your hair,
(your fingertips
the way you move)
                    the

painter of your voice—
beyond these elements

remarkably nothing is....therefore,lady
am i content should any
by me carven thing provoke
your gesture possibly or

any painting(for its own

reason)in your lips
slenderly should create one least smile
(shyly
if a poem should lift to
me the distinct country of your
eyes,gifted with green twilight)

# 186

Nobody wears a yellow
flower in his buttonhole
he is altogether a queer fellow
as young as he is old

when autumn comes,
who twiddles his white thumbs
and frisks down the boulevards

without his coat and hat

—(and i wonder just why that
should please him or i wonder what he does)

and why(at the bottom of this trunk,
under some dirty collars)only a
moment
(or
was it perhaps a year)ago i found staring

me in the face a dead yellow small rose

after all white horses are in bed

will you walking beside me,my very lady,
if scarcely the somewhat city
wiggles in considerable twilight

touch(now)with a suddenly unsaid

gesture lightly my eyes?
And send life out of me and the night
absolutely into me....a wise
and puerile moving of your arm will
do suddenly that

         will do
more than heroes beautifully in shrill
armour colliding on huge blue horses,
and the poets looked at them,and made verses,

through the sharp light cryingly as the knights flew.

touching you i say(it being Spring
and night)"let us go a very little beyond
the last road—there's something to be found"

and smiling you answer "everything
turns into something else,and slips away....
(these leaves are Thingish with moondrool
and i'm ever so very little afraid")
                                        i say
"along this particular road the moon if you'll
notice follows us like a big yellow dog.   You

don't believe?   look back.(Along the sand
behind us,a big yellow dog that's....now it's red
a big red dog that may be owned by who
knows)
          only turn a little your.   so.   And

there's the moon,there is something faithful and mad"

# 189

if i have made,my lady,intricate
imperfect various things chiefly which wrong
your eyes(frailer than most deep dreams are frail)
songs less firm than your body's whitest song
upon my mind—if i have failed to snare
the glance too shy—if through my singing slips
the very skilful strangeness of your smile
the keen primeval silence of your hair

—let the world say "his most wise music stole
nothing from death"—
                         you only will create
(who are so perfectly alive)my shame:
lady through whose profound and fragile lips
the sweet small clumsy feet of April came

into the ragged meadow of my soul.

# W

POEMS 190 TO 243

# 190

---

there are 6 doors.
Next door(but
four)gentlemen are trinightly entertained by a whore
who Talks in the daytime,when who

is asleep with only several
faces and a multitude of chins:next door
but three dwells;a(ghost)Who
screams Faintly always

who Is bluish;next
Door but two occupy a man
and his wife:Both very young noisily
who kiss throw silently things

Each at other(if not
quarrelling in a luxury of telescoped
languages)she smokes three
castles He looks jewish

,next door but One
a on Dirty bed Mangy from person Porous
sits years its of self fee(bly
Perpetually coughing And thickly spi)tting

But next door nobody
seems to live at present(l'on
parle de repapering;i
don't think so.maybe:somebody?)or,bedbugs

but mr can you maybe listen there's
me &
some people
and others please
don't
confuse.Some

people

's future is toothsome like
(they got
pockets full may take a littl
e nibble now And then
bite)candy

others
fly,their;puLLing:bright
futures
against the deep sky in

May mine's tou
ching this crump
led cap mumble some
thing to oh no
body will
(can you give
a)listen to
who may

you

be
any
how?
down
to
smoking
found
Butts

# 192

helves surling out of eakspeasies per(reel)hapsingly
proregress heandshe-ingly people
trickle curselaughgroping shrieks bubble
squirmwrithed staggerful unstrolls collaps ingly
flash a of-faceness stuck thumblike into pie
is traffic this recalls hat gestures bud
plumptumbling hand voices Eye Doangivuh suddenly immense impotently Eye Doancare Eye
And How replies the upsquirtingly careens
the to collide flatfooting with Wushyuhname
a girl-flops to the Geddup curb leans
carefully spewing into her own Shush Shame

as(out from behind Nowhere)creeps the deep thing
everybody sometimes calls morning

# 193

---

y is a WELL KNOWN ATHLETE'S BRIDE

(lullaby)
& z

= an infrafairy of floating
ultrawrists who
lullabylullaby

(I could have been
You,You
might have been I)
                    "?" quoth the

front;and there was yz
SHOT AND KILLED her
(in his arms)Self

                & Him
self in the hoe tell days are

teased:

        let(however)us
Walk very(therefore and)softly among one's own
memory(but)along perhaps the
By invisibilities spattered(or if

it may be socalled)memory
Of(without more ado about less
than nothing)

                2 boston
Dolls;found
with
Holes in each other

's lullaby and
other lulla wise by UnBroken
LULLAlullabyBY

                              the She-in-him with
the He-in-her(&

both all hopped
                    up)prettily
then which did
lie
Down,honestly

now who go(BANG(BANG

# 194

Lord John Unalive(having a fortune of fifteengrand
£
thanks to the socalled fact that maost faolks rally demannd
       canned
saounds)
gloats
upon the possession of quotes keltyer close
" "

aureally(yawning while all the dominoes)fall:down;in,rows

# 195

well)here's looking at ourselves

two solids in(all
one it)
solution(of
course you must shake well)

indolently dreaming puzzling

over that one
oh just thinking it over
(at that just supposing
we had met and just
but you know

supposing we

just had let it go at
that)that
seems important doesn't
it and
doesn't that seem
puzzling but we both might have found the solution

of that in

the importance of the
fact that(in spite of the fact
that i and that
you had carefully
ourselves decided what this cathedral ought to

look like)it doesn't look

at
all like what you
and what i(of course)
carefully had decided oh

no(but

# 196

---

Space being(don't forget to remember)Curved
(and that reminds me who said o yes Frost
Something there is which isn't fond of walls)

an electromagnetic(now I've lost
the)Einstein expanded Newton's law preserved
conTinuum(but we read that beFore)

of Course life being just a Reflex you
know since Everything is Relative or

to sum it All Up god being Dead(not to

mention inTerred)
                    LONG LIVE that Upwardlooking
Serene Illustrious and Beatific
Lord of Creation,MAN:
                        at a least crooking
of Whose compassionate digit,earth's most terrific

quadruped swoons into billiardBalls!

in a middle of a room
stands a suicide
sniffing a Paper rose
smiling to a self

"somewhere it is Spring and sometimes
people are in real:imagine
somewhere real flowers,but
I can't imagine real flowers for if I

could,they would somehow
not Be real"
(so he smiles
smiling)"but I will not

everywhere be real to
you in a moment"
The is blond
with small hands

"& everything is easier
than I had guessed everything would
be;even remembering the way who
looked at whom first,anyhow dancing"

(a moon swims out of a cloud
a clock strikes midnight
a finger pulls a trigger
a bird flies into a mirror)

i will cultivate within
me scrupulously the Inimitable which
is loneliness,these unique dreams
never shall soil their raiment

with phenomena:such
being a conduct worthy of

more ponderous
wishes or
hopes less
tall than mine"(opening the windows)

"and there is a philosophy" strictly at
which instant(leaped
into the

street)this deep immediate mask and
expressing "as for myself,because i
am slender and fragile
i borrow contact from that you and from

this you sensations,imitating a few fatally

exquisite"(pulling Its shawl carefully around
it)"things i mean the
Rain is no respecter of persons
the snow doesn't give a soft white
damn Whom it touches

a
 mong crum
            bling people(a
long ruined streets
hither and)softly

thither between(tumb
ling)
      houses(as
the kno

wing spirit prowls,its
nose winces
before a dissonance of

Rish and Foses)
               until
                  (finding one's self
at some distance from the
crooked town)a

harbour fools the sea(
while
       emanating the triple
starred

Hotel du Golf...that notable structure
or ideal edifice...situated or established
...far from the noise of waters
                              )one's

eye perceives
              (as the ego approaches)
painfully sterilized contours;
within

which
"ladies&gentlemen"
—under

glass—
are:
asking.

?each
oth?
er

rub,
!berq;
:uestions

# 200

the first president to be loved by his
bitterest enemies" is dead

the only man woman or child who wrote
a simple declarative sentence with seven grammatical
errors "is dead"
beautiful Warren Gamaliel Harding
"is" dead
he's
"dead"
if he wouldn't have eaten them Yapanese Craps

somebody might hardly never not have been unsorry,perhaps

# 201

---

"Gay" is the captivating cognomen of a Young Woman of
cambridge,mass.
to whom nobody seems to have mentioned ye olde
freudian wish;
when i contemplate her uneyes safely ensconced in thick
glass
you try if we are a gentleman not to think of(sh)

the world renowned investigator of paper sailors—
argonauta argo
harmoniously being with his probably most brilliant pupil
mated,
let us not deem it miraculous if their(so to speak)offspring
has that largo
appearance of somebody who was hectocotyliferously
propagated

when Miss G touched n.y. our skeleton stepped from his
cupboard
gallantly offering to demonstrate the biggest best bus-
iest city
and presently found himself rattling for that well known
suburb
the bronx(enlivening an otherwise dead silence with
harmless quips,out of Briggs by Kitty)

arriving in an exhausted condition,i purchased two bags
of lukewarm peanuts
with the dime which her mama had generously pro-
vided(despite courteous protestations)
and offering Miss Gay one(which she politely refused)set
out gaily for the hyenas
suppressing my frank qualms in deference to her not
inobvious perturbations

unhappily,the denizens of the zoo were that day inclined
    to be uncouthly erotic
more particularly the primates—from which with dignity
    square feet turned abruptly Miss Gay away:
"on the whole"(if you will permit a metaphor savouring
    slightly of the demotic)
Miss Gay had nothing to say to the animals and the
    animals had nothing to say to Miss Gay

during our return voyage,my pensive companion dimly
    remarked something about "stuffed
fauna" being "very interesting"...we also discussed the
    possibility of rain...
in distant proximity to a Y.W.c.a. she suddenly luffed
—thanking me;and(stating that she hoped we might "meet
    again

sometime")vanished,gunwale awash.  I thereupon loos-
    ened my collar
and dove for the nearest l;surreptitiously cogitating
the dictum of a new england sculptor(well on in life)re
    the helen moller
dancers,whom he considered "elevating—that is,if danc-
    ing CAN be elevating"

Miss(believe it or)Gay is a certain Young Woman un-
    acquainted with the libido
and pursuing a course of instruction at radcliffe college,
    cambridge,mass.
i try if you are a gentleman not to sense something un poco
    putrido
when we contemplate her uneyes safely ensconced in
    thick glass

# 202

---

buncha hardboil guys frum duh A.C. fulla
hooch kiddin eachudder bout duh clap an
talkin big how dey could kill
sixereight cops—"I sidesteps im an draws
back huly jeezus"—an—"my
specialty is takin fellers' goils away
frum dem"—"somebody hung uh gun on
Marcus"—"duh Swede rolls down tree flights an Sam
begins boxin im on duh
koib"—you
know
alotta sweet bull like dat
                              ...suddenly
i feels so lonely fer duh good ole days we
spent in '18 kickin duh guts outa dem
doity frogeaters an humpin duh
swell janes on
duh boollevares an wid tears
streamin down my face i hauls
out uh flask an offers it tuh duh whole gang accrost
duh table—"fellers
have some
on
me"—dey was petrified.

De room swung roun an crawled up into
itself,
an awful big light squoits down my spine like
i was dead er sumpn:next i

knows me(er
somebody is sittin in uh green
field watchin four crows drop into
sunset,playin uh busted harmonica

# 203

remarked Robinson Jefferson

to Injustice Taughed
your story is so interested

but you make me laft
welates Wouldwoe Washington
to Lydia E. McKinley

when Buch tooked out his C.O.D.
Abe tucks it up back inley
clamored Clever Rusefelt
to Theodore Odysseus Graren't

we couldn't free the negro
because he ant
but Coolitch wiped his valley forge

with Sitting Bull's T.P.
and the duckbilled platitude lays & lays

and Lays aytash unee

# 204

i sing of Olaf glad and big
whose warmest heart recoiled at war:
a conscientious object-or

his wellbbelovéd colonel(trig
westpointer most succinctly bred)
took erring Olaf soon in hand;
but—though an host of overjoyed
noncoms(first knocking on the head
him)do through icy waters roll
that helplessness which others stroke
with brushes recently employed
anent this muddy toiletbowl,
while kindred intellects evoke
allegiance per blunt instruments—
Olaf(being to all intents
a corpse and wanting any rag
upon what God unto him gave)
responds,without getting annoyed
"I will not kiss your fucking flag"

straightway the silver bird looked grave
(departing hurriedly to shave)

but—though all kinds of officers
(a yearning nation's blueeyed pride)
their passive prey did kick and curse
until for wear their clarion
voices and boots were much the worse,
and egged the firstclassprivates on
his rectum wickedly to tease
by means of skilfully applied
bayonets roasted hot with heat—
Olaf(upon what were once knees)
does almost ceaselessly repeat
"there is some shit I will not eat"

our president,being of which
assertions duly notified
threw the yellowsonofabitch
into a dungeon,where he died

Christ(of His mercy infinite)
i pray to see;and Olaf,too

preponderatingly because
unless statistics lie he was
more brave than me:more blond than you.

# 205

it)It will it
Will come(we
being
unwound & gone into the ground)but

though

with wormS eyes
writhe amor(Though through

our hearts hugely squirm
roots)us
          ly;though
hither nosing lymoles cru.Ising

thither:t,ouch soft-ly me and eye(you
leSs

)ly(un
        der the mi
                  croscopic world's

whens,wheels;wonders:
murders.cries:hopes;
houses,clouds.kisses,
lice;headaches:ifs.

)
 yet shall
our Not to
be

deciphered
selves

merely Continue to experience

a neverish subchemistry of
alWays
                )fiercely live whom on

Large Darkness And The Middle Of
The
E

a
r
t
H

myself,walking in Dragon st
one fine August
night,i just
happened to meet

"how do you do" she smiling
said "thought you
were earning your living
or probably dead"

so Jones was murdered by
a man named Smith and
we sailed on the
Leviathan

a light Out)
   & first of all foam

-like hair spatters creasing pillow
next everywhere hidinglyseek
no o god dear wait sh please o no O
3rd Findingest whispers understand
sobs bigly climb what(love being something possibly more intricate)i(breath
in breath)have nicknamed ecstasy and And

spills smile cheaply thick

—who therefore Thee(once and once only,Queen
among centuries universes between
Who out of deeplyness rose to undeath)

salute.  and having worshipped for my doom
pass ignorantly into sleep's bright land

# 208

---

when hair falls off and eyes blur And
thighs forget(when clocks whisper
and night shouts)When minds
shrivel and hearts grow brittler every
Instant(when of a morning Memory stands,
with clumsily wilted fingers
emptying youth colour and what was
into a dirtied glass)Pills for Ills
(a recipe against Laughing Virginity Death)

then dearest the
way trees are Made leaves
open Clouds take sun mountains
stand And oceans do Not sleep matters
nothing;then(then the only hands so to speak are
they always which creep budgingly over some
numbered face capable of a largest nonglance the
least unsmile
or whatever weeds feel and fish think of)

serene immediate silliest and whose
vast one function being to enter a Toy and
emerging(believably enlarged)make how
many stopped millions of female hard for their
millions of stopped male to look at(now
-fed infantile eyes drooling unmind
grim yessing childflesh perpetually acruise
and her quick way of slowly staring and such hair)
the Californian handpicked thrill mechanically
packed and released for all this very diminishing
vicarious ughhuh world(the pertly papped
muchmouthed)her way of beginningly finishing
(and such hair)the expensively democratic tyrannically
dumb
      Awake,chaos:we have napped.

# 210

don't cries to please my
mustn't broke)life Is
like that please stroke

for now stroke answers(but
now don't you're hurting o
Me please you're killing)death

is like now That please
squirtnowing for
o squirting we're replies(at

which now O fear turned o Now
handspring trans
forming it

self int
o eighteen)Don't
(for)Please(tnights,on whose for

eheads shone
eternal pleasedon't;
rising:from the Shall.

# 211

(one fine day)

let's take the train
for because dear

whispered again
in never's ear
(i'm tho thcared

giggling lithped now
we muthn't pleathe
don't as pop weird
up her hot ow

you hurt tho nithe
steered his big was)
thither to thence
swore many a vow
but both made sense

in when's haymow
with young fore'er
(oh & by the way
asked sis breath
of brud breathe
how is aunt death

did always teethe

# 212

---

what time is it i wonder never mind
consider rather heavenly things and but
the stars for instance everything is planned
next to that patch of darkness there's a what
is it oh yes chair but not Cassiopeia's

might those be stockings dribbling from the table
all which seemed sweet deep and inexplicable
not being dollars toenails or ideas
thoroughly's stolen(somewhere between

our unlighted hearts lust lurks
slovenly and homeless and when
a kiss departs our lips are made of thing

in beginning corners dawn smirks

and there's the moon,thinner than a watchspring

# 213

Wing Wong,uninterred at twice
fortyeight,succeeded in producing

sixtyfour maxims

whose)centripetal wisdom in
thirtytwo seconds centrifugally
is refuted by these(

particularly belonging to
a
retired
general)sixteen years

of rapid
animal whose swir
-ling(not too frequently
)skirt exhumes(which
buries again quick-

ly its
self in)while
a transparent blouse
even recklessly
juggles the jouncing
fruit of eager bosoms"
                                    Wing

Wong

# 214

a clown's smirk in the skull of a baboon
(where once good lips stalked or eyes firmly stirred)
my mirror gives me,on this afternoon;
i am a shape that can but eat and turd
ere with the dirt death shall him vastly gird,
a coward waiting clumsily to cease
whom every perfect thing meanwhile doth miss;
a hand's impression in an empty glove,
a soon forgotten tune,a house for lease.
I have never loved you dear as now i love

behold this fool who,in the month of June,
having of certain stars and planets heard,
rose very slowly in a tight balloon
until the smallening world became absurd;
him did an archer spy(whose aim had erred
never)and by that little trick or this
he shot the aeronaut down,into the abyss
—and wonderfully i fell through the green groove
of twilight,striking into many a piece.
I have never loved you dear as now i love

god's terrible face,brighter than a spoon,
collects the image of one fatal word;
so that my life(which liked the sun and the moon)
resembles something that has not occurred:
i am a birdcage without any bird,
a collar looking for a dog,a kiss
without lips;a prayer lacking any knees
but something beats within my shirt to prove
he is undead who,living,noone is.
I have never loved you dear as now i love.

Hell(by most humble me which shall increase)
open thy fire!for i have had some bliss
of one small lady upon earth above;
to whom i cry,remembering her face,
i have never loved you dear as now i love

come a little further—why be afraid—
here's the earliest star(have you a wish?)
touch me,
before we perish
(believe that not anything which has ever been
invented can spoil this or this instant)
kiss me a little:
the air
darkens and is alive—
o live with me in the fewness of
these colours;
alone who slightly
always are beyond the reach of death

and the English

# 216

you
in win
ter who sit
dying thinking
huddled behind dir
ty glass mind muddled
and cuddled by dreams(or some
times vacantly gazing through un
washed panes into a crisp todo of
murdering uncouth faces which pass rap
idly with their breaths.)"people are walking deaths
in this season" think "finality lives up
on them a little more openly than usual
hither,thither who briskly busily carry the as
tonishing & spontaneous & difficult ugliness
of themselves with a more incisive simplicity a
more intensively brutal futility" And sit
huddling dumbly behind three or two partly tran
sparent panes which by some loveless trick sepa
rate one stilled unmoving mind from a hun
dred doomed hurrying brains(by twos
or threes which fiercely rapidly
pass with their breaths)in win
ter you think,die slow
ly "toc tic" as i
have seen trees(in
whose black bod
ies leaves
hide

i met a man under the moon
on Sunday.
by way of saying
nothing he
smiled(but
just by the dirty collar of his

jacket were two glued uncarefully ears
in
that face a box of
skin lay eyes like
new tools)

whence i guessed that he also had climbed the pincian
to appreciate rome at nightfall;and because against this
wall his white sincere small
hands with their guessing fingers

did-not-move exquisitely
,like dead children
(if he had been playing a fiddle i had

been dancing:which is
why something about me reminded him of ourselves

as Nobody came slowly over the town

# 218

---

if there are any heavens my mother will(all by herself)have
one.  It will not be a pansy heaven nor
a fragile heaven of lilies-of-the-valley but
it will be a heaven of blackred roses

my father will be(deep like a rose
tall like a rose)

standing near my

swaying over her
(silent)
with eyes which are really petals and see

nothing with the face of a poet really which
is a flower and not a face with
hands
which whisper
This is my beloved my

                      (suddenly in sunlight
he will bow,

& the whole garden will bow)

memory believes
fragrance of a town(whose
dormers choke
and snore the steeples writhe with

rain)faces(at windows)do not
speak and are ghost or
huddled in the darkness of
cafés people drink

smile if here there(like lopsided
imaginations)
filled with newly murdered
flowers whispering barns

bulge a tiniest street or
three contains these prettiest
deaths without effort while
hungering churches(topped

with effigies of crowing
gold)nuzzle against summer
thunder(together)smell only
such blue slender hands of god

# 220

---

sunset)edges become swiftly
corners(Besides
which,i note how
fatally toward

twilight the a little
tilted streets spill lazily
multitudes out of final

towers;captured:in
the narrow light

of

inverno)this
is the season of
crumbling & folding
hopes,hark;feet(fEEt
f-e-e-t-noWheregoingaLwaYS

# 221

n(o)w

      the
how
    dis(appeared cleverly)world

iS Slapped:with;liGhtninG
!

 at
which(shal)lpounceupcrackw(ill)jumps

of
   THuNdeRB
        loSSo!M iN
-visiblya mongban(gedfrag-
ment ssky?wha tm)eani ngl(essNessUn
rolli)ngl yS troll s(who leO v erd)oma insCol

Lide.!high
       n , o ; w :
               theraIncomIng

o all the roofs roar
          drownInsound(
&
(we(are like)dead
      )Whoshout(Ghost)atOne(voiceless)O
ther or im)
   pos
   sib(ly as
   leep)
     But l!ook—
      s

U

　　　n:starT birDs(lEAp)Openi ng
t hing ; s(
—sing
　　　)all are aLl(cry alL See)o(ver All)Th(e grEEn

?eartH)N,ew

# 222

twi-
        is -Light bird
ful
-ly dar
kness eats

a distance a
c(h)luck
(l)ing of just bells (touch)ing
?mind

(moon begins The
)
now,est hills er dream;new
.oh if

        when:
&
a
nd O impercept i bl

# 223

thou

        firsting a hugeness of twi
                        -light
pale
     beyond soft-
liness than dream more sing

(buoyant & who
silently shall to rea- disa)

ular,

       (ppear ah!Star
                whycol

our
    ed
shy lurch small invin

cible nod oc
cul
   t ke
ylike writhe of brea

            Thing

# 224

if i love You
(thickness means
worlds inhabited by roamingly
stern bright faeries

if you love
me)distance is mind carefully
luminous with innumerable gnomes
Of complete dream

if we love each(shyly)
other,what clouds do or Silently
Flowers resembles beauty
less than our breathing

somewhere i have never travelled,gladly beyond
any experience,your eyes have their silence:
in your most frail gesture are things which enclose me,
or which i cannot touch because they are too near

your slightest look easily will unclose me
though i have closed myself as fingers,
you open always petal by petal myself as Spring opens
(touching skilfully,mysteriously)her first rose

or if your wish be to close me,i and
my life will shut very beautifully,suddenly,
as when the heart of this flower imagines
the snow carefully everywhere descending;

nothing which we are to perceive in this world equals
the power of your intense fragility:whose texture
compels me with the colour of its countries,
rendering death and forever with each breathing

(i do not know what it is about you that closes
and opens;only something in me understands
the voice of your eyes is deeper than all roses)
nobody,not even the rain,has such small hands

# 226

is there a flower(whom
i meet anywhere
able to be and seem
so quite softly as your hair

what bird has perfect fear
(of suddenly me)like these
first deepest rare
quite who are your eyes

(shall any dream
come a more millionth mile
shyly to its doom
than you will smile)

my darling since
you and
i are thoroughly haunted by
what neither is any
echo of dream nor
any flowering of any

echo(but the echo
of the flower of

Dreaming)somewhere behind us
always trying(or sometimes trying under
us)to is it
find somehow(but O gracefully)a
we,entirely whose least

breathing may surprise
ourselves
          —let's then
despise what is not courage my

darling(for only Nobody knows
where truth grows why
birds fly and
especially who the moon is.

# 228

because i love you)last night

clothed in sealace
appeared to me
your mind drifting
with chuckling rubbish
of pearl weed coral and stones;

lifted,and(before my
eyes sinking)inward,fled;softly
your face smile breasts gargled
by death:drowned only

again carefully through deepness to rise
these your wrists
thighs feet hands

poising
          to again utterly disappear;
rushing gently swiftly creeping
through my dreams last
night,all of your
body with its spirit floated
(clothed only in

the tide's acute weaving murmur

# 229

if you and i awakening

discover that(somehow
in the dark)this world has been
Picked,like a piece
of clover,from the green meadow of

time

lessness;quietly
                  turning
toward me the
guessable mirrors which your eyes are

You will communicate a little

more than twice all that
so
gently
while we were asleep while
we were each other disappeared:but i

slightly

smiling,
gradually shall reenter the

singular kingdom

(sleep)
        .while some
thing else
kisses busily
a
memory,which how exquisitely
flutters in

the cornerless tomorrow

# 230

lady will you come with me into
the extremely little house of
my mind. Clocks strike. The

moon's round,through the window

as you see and really i have no
servants. We could almost live

at the top of these stairs,there's a free
room. We almost could go(you
and i)into a together whitely big
there is but if so or so

slowly i opened the window a
most tinyness,the moon(with white wig
and polished buttons)would take you away

—and all the clocks would run down the next day.

# 231

when rain whom fear
not children but men
speaks(among leaves Easily
through voices womenlike telling

of death love earth dark)

and thousand
thrusts squirms stars
Trees,swift each with its

Own motion deeply to wickedly

comprehend the innocently Doomed
brief all which somewhere is

fragrantly,

arrive
        (when
Rain comes;
predicating forever,assuming
the laughter of afterwards—
i spirally understand

What

touching means
or What does a hand
with your hair
in my imagination

# 232

item:is

    Clumsily with of
what manshaped whimpered how
                    girllike
laughtering blocks when

builds
its invisibly skil
ful toyTown
which upups to dowNdown
(and only where remembers

look,
      this was of a child
's shy foot among cool ferns

)
 therefore togethering our

wholly lives Givehurling
with your my most
:locking

          foreverfully

blend
      we a universe of gulls'
drift Of thickly
             starhums wherefore

& wormSmile eternal;quite
perhaps as sternly
much not life nor stop as
a tear is darker than a mile.

i'd think "wonder

if" if
i were a
child "we can see a bat in this
twilight")
            there one is

look

how it goes      like      a dream

(and between houses,really a kind of
mouse)but he has little wings
and here's my
hotel this is the
door(opening it i

think things
which
were supposed to
be out of my
reach
        ,they are like
jam on the shelf everybody guessed

was too high

look

        (it's back again      there      therehere
And)i say "won't you"(remembering)
knowing that you
are afraid "go first" of dreams and little

bats & mice(and

                    you,
you say "let's" going in
"take
hands" smiling "coming up
these dark stairs.

breathe with me this fear
(which beyond night shall go)
remembering only dare
(Wholly consider how

these immaculate thin
things half daemon half
tree among sunset dream
acute from root to leaf

but should voices(whom lure
an eagerest strict flame)
demand the metaphor
of our projectile am

tell such to murder time
(forgetting what's to know
wholly imagining fire)
only consider How

# 235

granted the all
                    saving our young kiss only
must unexist,solemnly and per rules
apparelling its soullessness by lonely
antics of ridiculous molecules)

nakedest(aiming for hugely the
ignorant most precise essential flame
never which waked)& perfectingly We

dive

        out of tinying time
                    (into supreme

Now:
        feeling memory shrink from such brief
selves as fiercely seek findingly new
textures of actual cool stupendous is

nor may truth opening encompass true)
while your contriving fate,my sharpening life

are(behind each no)touching every yes

# 236

speaking of love(of
which Who knows the
meaning;or how dreaming
becomes

if your heart's mine)i
guess a grassblade
Thinks beyond or
around(as poems are

made)Our picking it. this
caress that laugh
both quickly signify
life's only half(through

deep weather then
or none let's feel
all)mind in mind flesh
In flesh succeeding disappear

# 237

---

be unto love as rain is unto colour;create
me gradually(or as these emerging now
hills invent the air)
                    breathe simply my each how
my trembling where my still unvisible when.   Wait

if i am not heart,because at least i beat
—always think i am gone like a sun which must go
sometimes,to make an earth gladly seem firm for you:
remember(as those pearls more than surround this throat)

i wear your dearest fears beyond their ceaselessness

(nor has a syllable of the heart's eager dim
enormous language loss or gain from blame or praise)
but many a thought shall die which was not born of dream
while wings welcome the year and trees dance(and i guess

though wish and world go down,one poem yet shall swim

# 238

so standing,our eyes filled with wind,and the
whining rigging over us,i implore you to
notice how the keen ship lifts(skilfully
like some bird which is all birds but more fleet)
herself against the air—and whose do you
suppose possibly are certain hands,terse
and invisible,with large first new stars
knitting the structure of distinct sunset

driving white spikes of silence into joists
hewn from hugest colour
                        (and which night hoists
miraculously above the always
beyond such wheres and fears or any when
unwondering immense directionless
horizon)
          —do you perhaps know these workmen?

# 239

nothing is more exactly terrible than
to be alone in the house,with somebody and
with something)
                    You are gone.  there is laughter

and despair impersonates a street

i lean from the window,behold ghosts,
                                      a man
hugging a woman in a park.  Complete.

and slightly(why?or lest we understand)
slightly i am hearing somebody
coming up stairs,carefully
(carefully climbing carpeted flight after
carpeted flight.  in stillness,climbing
the carpeted stairs of terror)

and continually i am seeing something

inhaling gently a cigarette(in a mirror

structure,miraculous challenge,devout am

upward deep most invincible unthing
—stern sexual timelessness,outtowering
this noisy impotence of not and same

answer,beginning,ecstasy,to dare:
prouder than all mountains,more than all
oceans various
                              and while everywhere
beneath thee and about thyself a small
hoping insect,humanity,achieves
(moult beyond difficult moult)amazing doom
who standest as thou hast stood and thou shalt stand.

Nor any dusk but kneelingly believes
thy secret and each morning stoops to blend

her star with what huge merciful forms presume

# 241

put off your faces,Death:for day is over
(and such a day as must remember he
who watched unhands describe what mimicry,

with angry seasalt and indignant clover
marrying to themselves Life's animals)

but not darkness shall quite outmarch forever
—and i perceive,within transparent walls
how several smoothly gesturing stars are clever
to persuade even silence:therefore wonder

opens a gate;the prisoner dawn embraces

hugely some few most rare perfectly dear
(and worlds whirl beyond worlds:immortal yonder
collidingly absorbs eternal near)

day being come,Love,put on your faces

# 242

here is the ocean,this is moonlight:say
that both precisely beyond either were—
so in darkness ourselves go,mind in mind

which is the thrilling least of all(for love's
secret supremely clothes herself with day)
i mean,should any curious dawn discuss
our mingling spirits,you would disappear
unreally;as this planet(understand)

forgets the entire and perpetual sea

—but if yourself consider wonderful
that your(how luminous)life toward twilight will
dissolve reintegrate beckon through me,
i think it is less wonderful than this

only by you my heart always moves

# 243

but if a living dance upon dead minds
why,it is love;but at the earliest spear
of sun perfectly should disappear
moon's utmost magic,or stones speak or one
name control more incredible splendor than
our merely universe,love's also there:
and being here imprisoned,tortured here
love everywhere exploding maims and blinds
(but surely does not forget,perish,sleep
cannot be photographed,measured;disdains
the trivial labelling of punctual brains...
—Who wields a poem huger than the grave?
from only Whom shall time no refuge keep
though all the weird worlds must be opened?
                                    )Love

# No Thanks

POEMS 244 TO 293

# 244

o
sure)but
nobody unders(no
but Rully yes i
know)but what it comes

to(listen you don't have to

i mean Reely)but(no listen don't
be sil why sure)i mean the(o
well ughhuh sure why not yuh course yeh well
naturally i und certain i o posi but

i know sure that's)but listen here's

(correct you said it yeah)but
listen but(it's Rilly yeh
ughhuh yuh)i know

(o sure i

know yes
of

course)but what i mean is Nobody Understands Her RERLY

# 245

when muckers pimps and tratesmen
 delivered are of vicians
 and all the world howls stadesmen
 beware of politisions

 beware of folks with missians
 to turn us into rissions
 and blokes with ammunicions
 who tend to make incitions

 and pity the fool who cright
 god help me it aint no ews
 eye like the steak all ried
 but eye certainly hate the juse

# 246

"let's start a magazine

to hell with literature
we want something redblooded

lousy with pure
reeking with stark
and fearlessly obscene

but really clean
get what I mean
let's not spoil it
let's make it serious

something authentic and delirious
you know something genuine like a mark
in a toilet

graced with guts and gutted
with grace"

squeeze your nuts and open your face

he does not have to feel because he thinks
(the thoughts of others,be it understood)
he does not have to think because he knows
(that anything is bad which you think good)

because he knows,he cannot understand
(why Jones don't pay me what he knows he owes)
because he cannot understand,he drinks
(and he drinks and he drinks and he drinks and)

not bald.   (Coughs.)   Two pale slippery small eyes

balanced upon one broken babypout
(pretty teeth wander into which and out
of)Life,dost Thou contain a marvel than
this death named Smith less strange?
Married and lies

afraid;aggressive and:American

# 248

---

this little
pair had a little scare
right in the middle of a bed bed
bed)when each other courted both
was very very thwarted(and
when which was aborted
what was dead dead dead)

whereupon mary
quite contrary didn't
die
(may be seen to inexactly pass and unprecisely
to repass where
flesh is heiry montparnasse
is goosed by raspail).

But he turned into a fair
y!a fair
y!!a
fair
y!!!
but she turned into a fair-y(and
it seems to be doing nicely

o pr
  gress verily thou art m
  mentous superc
  lossal hyperpr
  digious etc i kn
  w & if you d

n't why g
  to yonder s
  called newsreel s
  called theatre & with your
  wn eyes beh

ld The
        (The president The
        president of The president
        of the The)president of

        the(united The president of the
        united states The president of the united
        states of The President Of The)United States

        Of America unde negant redire quemquam supp
sedly thr

w
  i
   n
    g
     a
      b
        aseball

may i feel said he
(i'll squeal said she
just once said he)
it's fun said she

(may i touch said he
how much said she
a lot said he)
why not said she

(let's go said he
not too far said she
what's too far said he
where you are said she)

may i stay said he
(which way said she
like this said he
if you kiss said she

may i move said he
is it love said she)
if you're willing said he
(but you're killing said she

but it's life said he
but your wife said she
now said he)
ow said she

(tiptop said he
don't stop said she
oh no said he)
go slow said she

(cccome?said he
ummm said she)
you're divine!said he
(you are Mine said she)

kumrads die because they're told)
kumrads die before they're old
(kumrads aren't afraid to die
kumrads don't
and kumrads won't
believe in life)and death knows whie

(all good kumrads you can tell
by their altruistic smell
moscow pipes good kumrads dance)
kumrads enjoy
s.freud knows whoy
the hope that you may mess your pance

every kumrad is a bit
of quite unmitigated hate
(travelling in a futile groove
god knows why)
and so do i
(because they are afraid to love

# 252

worshipping Same
they squirm and they spawn
and a world is for them,them;whose
death's to be born)

his birth is their fear is their blind fear
—haunts all unsleep
this cry of one fiend,
a thousand dreams thick

(cringing they brood
breeding they wince)
his laugh is a million griefs wide(it
shall bury much stench)

and a hundred joys high are such shoulders
as cowards will scheme
to harness:let all
unfools of unbeing

set traps for his heart,
lay snares for his feet
(who wanders through only white darkness
who moves in black light

dancing isn'ts on why,digging bridges with mirrors
from whispers to stars;
climbing silence for ifs
diving under because)

only who'll say
"and this be my fame,
the harder the wind blows the
taller i am"

# 253

that which we who're alive in spite of mirrors
(have died beyond the clock)we,of ourselves

who more a part are(less who are aware)

than of my books could even be your shelves
(that which we die for;not when or unless
if or to prove,imperfectly or since

but through spontaneous deft strictly horrors

which stars may not observe;while roses wince)
that which we die for lives(may never cease
views with smooth vigilant perpetual eyes
each exact victim,how he does not stir)

O love,my love!soul clings and heart conceives

and mind leaps(and that which we die for lives
as wholly as that which we live for dies)

# 254

little man
(in a hurry
full of an
important worry)
halt stop forget relax

wait

(little child
who have tried
who have failed
who have cried)
lie bravely down

sleep

big rain
big snow
big sun
big moon
(enter

us)

# 255

sonnet entitled how to run the world)

A always don't there B being no such thing
for C can't casts no shadow D drink and

E eat of her voice in whose silence the music of spring
lives F feel opens but shuts understand
G gladly forget little having less

with every least each most remembering
H highest fly only the flag that's furled

(sestet entitled grass is flesh or swim
who can and bathe who must or any dream
means more than sleep as more than know means guess)

I item i immaculately owe
dying one life and will my rest to these

children building this rainman out of snow

# 256

brIght

bRight s??? big
(soft)

soft near calm
(Bright)
calm st?? holy

(soft briGht deep)
yeS near sta? calm star big yEs
alone
(wHo

Yes
near deep whO big alone soft near
deep calm deep
????Ht ?????T)
Who(holy alone)holy(alone holy)alone

# 257

most(people

simply

can't)
won't(most
parent people mustn't

shouldn't)most daren't

(sortof people well
youknow kindof)
aint

&

even
(not having
most ever lived

people always)don't

die(becoming most
buried unbecomingly
very

by

most)people

# 258

Jehovah buried,Satan dead,
do fearers worship Much and Quick;
badness not being felt as bad,
itself thinks goodness what is meek;
obey says toc,submit says tic,
Eternity's a Five Year Plan:
if Joy with Pain shall hang in hock
who dares to call himself a man?

go dreamless knaves on Shadows fed,
your Harry's Tom,your Tom is Dick;
while Gadgets murder squawk and add,
the cult of Same is all the chic;
by instruments,both span and spic,
are justly measured Spic and Span:
to kiss the mike if Jew turn kike
who dares to call himself a man?

loudly for Truth have liars pled,
their heels for Freedom slaves will click;
where Boobs are holy,poets mad,
illustrious punks of Progress shriek;
when Souls are outlawed,Hearts are sick,
Hearts being sick,Minds nothing can:
if Hate's a game and Love's a fuck
who dares to call himself a man?

King Christ,this world is all aleak;
and lifepreservers there are none:
and waves which only He may walk
Who dares to call Himself a man.

# 259

into a truly
curving form
enters my
soul

feels all small
facts dissolved
by the lewd guess
of fabulous immensity

the sky screamed
the sun died)
the ship lifts
on seas of iron

breathing height eating
steepness the
ship climbs
murmuring silver mountains

which
disappear(and
only
was night

and through only this night a
mightily form moves
whose passenger and whose
pilot my spirit is

# 260

---

exit a kind of unkindness exit

little
mr Big
notbusy
Busi
ness notman

(!ye
galleon
wilts
b:
   e;n,d

i
 ng
like like,like bad,like
candy:& you

are dead
you captain)

Memo 1
wife in impossibly
hell Memo
1 son
in improbably yale

little joe gould has lost his teeth and doesn't know where
to find them(and found a secondhand set which click)little
gould used to amputate his appetite with bad brittle
candy but just(nude eel)now little joe lives on air

Harvard Brevis Est for Handkerchief read Papernapkin no laundry
bills likes People preferring Negroes Indians Youse
n.b. ye twang of little joe(yankee)gould irketh sundry
who are trying to find their minds(but never had any to lose)

and a myth is as good as a smile but little joe gould's quote oral
history unquote might(publishers note)be entitled a wraith's
progress or mainly awash while chiefly submerged or an amoral
morality sort-of-aliveing by innumerable kind-of-deaths

(Amérique Je T'Aime and it may be fun to be fooled
but it's more fun to be more to be fun to be little joe gould)

sh estiffl
ystrut sal
lif san
dbut sth

epoutin(gWh.ono:w
s li psh ergo
wnd ow n,
                r
Eve

aling 2 a
-sprout eyelands)sin
uously&them&twi
tching,begins

unununun?
butbutbut??
tonton???
ing????

—Out-&
        steps;which
flipchucking
.grins
gRiNdS

d is app ea r in gly
eyes grip live loop croon mime
nakedly hurl asquirm the
dip&giveswoop&swoon&ingly

seethe firm swirl hips whirling climb to
GIVE
(yoursmine mineyours yoursmine
!
i()t)

# 263

---

floatfloafloflf
lloloa
tatoatloatf loat fl oat
f loatI ngL

y

&fris
klispin
glyT
　　w
　　　irlErec

t,
;d
;:a:
nC.eda:Nci;ddaanncciinn

(GlY)

a
　nda
　　　n-saint
dance!Dan
Sai ntd anc

&e&

—cupidoergosum
spun=flash
omiepsicronlonO—
megaeta?
            p
                aul D-as-in-tip-toe r

apeR

out of a supermetamathical subpreincestures
pooped universe(of croons canned
à la vallee and preserved goldfishian gestures)
suddenly sally rand

handsomely who did because she could what the movies try
to do because they can't i mean move
yes sir she jes was which the radio aint(proov
-ing that the quickness of the fand intrigues the fly)

for know all men($\chi\alpha\acute{\iota}\rho\varepsilon\tau\varepsilon$)
as it was in the beginning it(rejoice)
was and ever shall be nor every partialness beats one entirety
neither may shadow down flesh neither may vibration create
        voice

if therefore among foul pains appears an if emerges a joy let
's thank indecent
god p.s. the most successful b.o.fully speaking concession
        at the recent
world's fair was the paytoilet

# 265

theys sO alive
       (who is
             ?niggers)

      Not jes
      livin
      not Jes alive But
      So alive(they

    s
    born alive)
   some folks aint born
   somes born dead an
   somes born alive(but

    niggers
   is
  all
  born
 so
Alive)

   ump-A-tum
       ;tee-die

    uM-tuM
      tidl
       -id

    umptyumpty(OO——

             !

    ting
   Bam-
 :do)
,chippity.

death(having lost)put on his universe
and yawned:it looks like rain
(they've played for timelessness
with chips of when)
that's yours;i guess
you'll have to loan me pain
to take the hearse,
see you again.

Love(having found)wound up such pretty toys
as themselves could not know:
the earth tinily whirls;
while daisies grow
(and boys and girls
have whispered thus and so)
and girls with boys
to bed will go,

does yesterday's perfection seem not quite

so clever as the pratfall of a clown
(should stink of failure more than wars of feet

all things whose slendering sweetness touched renown)
suddenly themselves if all dreams unmake
(when in a most smashed unworld stands unslain

he which knows not if any anguish struck
how thin a ghost so deep and he might live)
yes,partly nor some edgeless star could give
that anguish room;but likes it only this

eternal mere one bursting soul
                              why,then

comes peace unto men who are always men
while a man shall which a god sometimes is

I the lost shoulders S the empty spine

how dark and single,where he ends,the earth
(whose texture feels of pride and loneliness
alive like some dream giving more than all
life's busy little dyings may possess)

how sincere large distinct and natural
he comes to his disappearance;as a mind
full without fear might faithfully lie down
to so much sleep they only understand

enormously which fail—look:with what ease
that bright how plural tide measures her guest
(as critics will upon a poet feast)

meanwhile this ghost goes under,his drowned girth
are mountains;and beyond all hurt of praise
the unimaginable night not known

here's to opening and upward,to leaf and to sap
and to your(in my arms flowering so new)
self whose eyes smell of the sound of rain

and here's to silent certainly mountains;and to
a disappearing poet of always,snow
and to morning;and to morning's beautiful friend
twilight(and a first dream called ocean)and

let must or if be damned with whomever's afraid
down with ought with because with every brain
which thinks it thinks,nor dares to feel(but up
with joy;and up with laughing and drunkenness)

here's to one undiscoverable guess
of whose mad skill each world of blood is made
(whose fatal songs are moving in the moon

# 270

---

(b
  eLl
    s?
      bE

-ginningly)come-swarm:faces
ar;rive go.faces a(live)
sob bel
ls

(pour wo
      (things)
          men
             selves-them

inghurl)bangbells(yawnchurches
suck people)reel(dark-
ly)whirling
in

(b
  ellSB
     el
      Ls)

-to sun(crash).Streets
glit
ter
a,strut:do;colours;are:m,ove

o im
    -pos-
       sibl
         y

(ShoutflowereD
flowerish boom
b el Lsb El l
s!cry)

(be
    llsbe
          lls)
              b
              (be
                  llsbell)
                        ells
                          (sbells)

love is a place
& through this place of
love move
(with brightness of peace)
all places

yes is a world
& in this world of
yes live
(skilfully curled)
all worlds

# 272

at dusk
        just when
the Light is filled with birds
seriously
i begin

to climb the best hill,
driven by black wine.
a village does not move behind
my eye

the windmills are
silent
their flattened arms
complain steadily against the west

one Clock dimly cries
nine,i stride among the vines
(my heart pursues
against the little moon

a here and there lark
                        who;rises,
and;droops
as if upon a thread invisible)

A graveyard dreams through its
cluttered and brittle emblems,or
a field(and i pause among
the smell of minute mown lives)oh

my spirit you
tumble
climb
        and mightily fatally

i remark how through deep lifted
fields Oxen distinctly move,a
yellowandbluish cat(perched why
Curvingly at this)window;yes

women sturdily meander in my
mind,woven by always upon
sunset,
crickets within me whisper

whose erect blood finally
trembles,emerging to perceive
buried in cliff
                    precisely

at the Ending of this road,
a candle in a shrine:
its puniest flame persists
shaken by the sea

birds(
        here,inven
ting air
U
)sing

tw
iligH(
t's
        v
            va
                vas(
    vast

ness.Be)look
now
        (come
soul;
&:and

who
        s)e
            voi
c
es
(
 are
        ar
            a

# 274

mouse)Won
derfully is
anyone else entirely who doesn't
move(Moved more suddenly than)whose

tiniest smile?may Be
bigger than the fear of all
hearts never which have
(Per

haps)loved(or than
everyone that will Ever love)we
've
hidden him in A leaf

and,
Opening
beautiful earth
put(only)a Leaf among dark

ness.sunlight's
thenlike?now
Disappears
some

thing(silent:
madeofimagination
;the incredible soft)ness
(his ears(eyes

# 275

go(perpe)go

(tu)to(al
adve

nturin
g p
article

s of s
ini
sterd
exte

ri)go to(ty)the(om
nivorou salways lugbrin
g ingseekfindlosin g
motilities
are)go to

the
ant
(al
ways

alingwaysing)
go to the ant thou go
(inging)

to the
ant,thou ant-

eater

                              r-p-o-p-h-e-s-s-a-g-r
                    who
        a)s w(e loo)k
        upnowgath
                    PPEGORHRASS
                              eringint(o-
            aThe):l
                eA
                    !p:
        S
                                              a
                        (r
            rIvInG              .gRrEaPsPhOs)
                                        to
        rea(be)rran(com)gi(e)ngly
        ,grasshopper;

moOn Over tOwns moOn
whisper
less creature huge grO
pingness

whO perfectly whO
flOat
newly alOne is
dreamest

oNLY THE MooN o
VER ToWNS
SLoWLY SPRoUTING SPIR
IT

love's function is to fabricate unknownness

(known being wishless;but love,all of wishing)
though life's lived wrongsideout,sameness chokes oneness
truth is confused with fact,fish boast of fishing

and men are caught by worms(love may not care
if time totters,light droops,all measures bend
nor marvel if a thought should weigh a star
—dreads dying least;and less,that death should end)

how lucky lovers are(whose selves abide
under whatever shall discovered be)
whose ignorant each breathing dares to hide
more than most fabulous wisdom fears to see

(who laugh and cry)who dream,create and kill
while the whole moves;and every part stands still:

# 279

---

Do.
omful
relaxing

-ly)i
downrise outwrithein-
ing upfall and

Am the glad deep the living from nowh
-ere(!firm!)exp-
anding,am a fe

-rvently(susta-
inin
-gness Am

root air rock day)
:you;
smile,hands

(an-
onymo
-Us

Spring(side

walks are)is
most(windows where blaze

naLOVEme
crazily
ships

bulge hearts by
darts pierced lazily writhe
lurch faceflowers stutter
treebodies wobbly-

ing thing
-birds)sing-
u
(cities are houses
people are flies who

buzz on)-lar(windows called sidewalks
of houses called cities)spring
most singular-
ly(cities are houses are)is(are owned

by a m- by
a -n by a
-oo-

is old as
the jews are a moon is

as round as)Death

what a proud dreamhorse pulling(smoothloomingly)through
(stepp)this(ing)crazily seething of this
raving city screamingly street wonderful

flowers And o the Light thrown by Them opens

sharp holes in dark places paints eyes touches hands with newness and these startled whats are a(piercing clothes
       thoughts kiss
-ing wishes bodies)squirm-of-frightened shy are whichs small
its hungry for Is for Love Spring thirsty for happens
only and beautiful
           there is a ragged beside the who limps
man crying silence upward
              —to have tasted Beautiful to have
   known
Only to have smelled Happens—skip dance kids hop point at
red blue yellow violet white orange green-
ness

     o what a proud dreamhorse moving(whose feet
almost walk air).  now who stops. Smiles.he
                stamps

# 282

this mind made war
being generous
this heart could dare)
unhearts can less

unminds must fear
because and why
what filth is here
unlives do cry

on him they shat
they shat encore
he laughed and spat
(this life could dare

freely to give
as gives a friend
not those who slave
unselves to lend

for hope of hope
must coo or boo
may strut or creep
ungenerous who

ape deftly aims
they dare not share)
such make their names
(this poet made war

whose naught and all
sun are and moon
come fair come foul
he goes alone

daring to dare
for joy of joy)
what stink is here
unpoets do cry

unfools unfree
undeaths who live
nor shall they be
and must they have

at him they fart
they fart full oft
(with mind with heart
he spat and laughed

with self with life
this poet arose
nor hate nor grief
can go where goes

this whyless soul
a loneliest road
who dares to stroll
almost this god

this surely dream
perhaps this ghost)
humbly and whom
for worst or best

(and proudly things
only which grow
and the rain's wings
the birds of snow

things without name
beyond because
things over blame
things under praise

glad things or free
truly which live
always shall be
may never have)

do i salute
(by moon by sun
i deeply greet
this fool and man

sometimes
     in)Spring a someone will lie(glued
among familiar things newly which are
transferred with dusk)wondering why this star
does not fall into his mind
        feeling
throughout ignorant disappearing me
hurling vastness of love(sometimes in Spring
somewhere between what is and what may be
unknown most secret i will breathe such crude
perfection as divides by timelessness
that heartbeat)
     mightily forgetting all
which will forget him(emptying our soul
of emptiness)priming at every pore
a deathless life with magic until peace
outthunders silence.
     And(night climbs the air

# 284

when
      from a sidewalk
            out of(blown never quite to
-gether by large sorry)creatures out
of(clumsily shining out of)instru-
ments,waltzing;undigestibly:groans.bounce

!o-ras-ourh an-dorg-an ble-at-ssw-ee-t-noth ings orarancidhurd
ygurdygur glingth umpssomet hings(whi,le sp,arrow,s wince
among those skeletons of these trees)
               when
                    sunbeams loot
furnished rooms through whose foul windows absurd
clouds cruise nobly ridiculous skies

(the;mselve;s a;nd scr;a;tch-ing lousy full.of.rain
beggars yaw:nstretchy:awn)
          then,
              o my love
                  ,then
it's Spring
     immortal Always & lewd shy New

and upon the beyond imagining spasm rise
we
     you-with-me
          around(me)you
              IYou

# 285

---

silent unday by silently not night

did the great world(in darkly taking rain)
drown,beyond sound
            down(slowly
                    beneath
                          sight
fall
    ing)fall
        ing through touch
                less stillness(seized

among what ghostly nevers of again)
silent not night by silently unday
life's bright less dwindled to a leastful most
under imagination.  When(out of sheer

nothing)came a huger than fear a

white with madness wind and broke oceans and tore
mountains from their sockets and strewed the black air
with writhing alive skies—and in death's place
new fragrantly young earth space opening was.
Were your eyes:lost,believing;hushed with when

# 286

come(all you mischief-
hatchers hatch
mischief)all you

guilty
   scamper(you bastards throw dynamite)
   let knowings magic
   with bright credos each divisible fool

(life imitate gossip fear unlife
mean
 -ness,and
   to succeed in not
      dying)

Is will still occur;birds disappear
becomingly:a thunderbolt compose poems
not because harm symmetry
   earthquakes starfish(but
   because nobody
      can sell the Moon to The)moon

# 287

be of love(a little)
More careful
Than of everything
guard her perhaps only

A trifle less
(merely beyond how very)
closely than
Nothing,remember love by frequent

anguish(imagine
Her least never with most
memory)give entirely each
Forever its freedom

(Dare until a flower,
understanding sizelessly sunlight
Open what thousandth why and
discover laughing)

# 288

much i cannot)
tear up the world:& toss
it away;or
cause one causeless cloud to purely grow

but,never
doubt my weakness
makes more than most
strength(less than these how

less than least flowers of rain)thickly
i fail slenderly i
win(like touch all stars or
to live in the moon

a while)and shall
carve time so we'll before
what's death
come(in one bed.

# 289

move
deeply,rain
(dream hugely)wish
firmly.  splendidly advancing colour

strike
into form
(actually)realness
kill

(make
strangely)known(establish
new)come,what
Being!open us open

our
selves.  create
(suddenly announce:hurl)
blind full steep love

if night's mostness(and whom did merely day
close)
      opens
          if more than silence silent are more
flowering than stars whitely births of mind

if air is throbbing prayers whom kneeling eyes
(until perfectly their imperfect gaze
climbs this steep fragrance of eternity)
world by than worlds immenser world will pray

so(unlove disappearing)only your
less than guessed more than beauty begins the
most not imagined life adventuring
who would feel if spring's least breathing should cause
a colour
        and i do not know him
                    (and

while behind death's death whenless voices sing
everywhere your selves himself recognize)

# 291

---

reason let others give and realness bring—
ask the always impossible of me
and shall who wave among your deepening
thighs a greedier wand than even death's

what beneath breathing selves transported are
into how suddenly so huge a home
(only more than immeasurable dream
wherelessly spiralling)beyond time's sky

and through this opening universe will wraiths
of doom rush(which all ghosts of life became)
and does our fatally unshadowing fate
put on one not imaginable star

:then a small million of dark voices sing
against the awful mystery of light

# 292

morsel miraculous and meaningless

secret on luminous whose selves and lives
imperishably feast all timeless souls

(the not whose spiral hunger may appease
what merely riches of our pretty world
sweetly who flourishes,swiftly which fails

but out of serene perfectly Nothing hurled
into young Now entirely arrives
gesture past fragrance fragrant;a than pure

more signalling of singular most flame
and surely poets only understands)
honour this loneliness of even him

who fears and eyes lifts lifting hopes and hands
—nourish my failure with thy freedom:star

isful beckoningly fabulous crumb

conceive a man,should he have anything
would give a little more than it away

(his autumn's winter being summer's spring
who moved by standing in november's may)
from whose(if loud most howish time derange

the silent whys of such a deathlessness)
remembrance might no patient mind unstrange
learn(nor could all earth's rotting scholars guess
that life shall not for living find the rule)

and dark beginnings are his luminous ends
who far less lonely than a fire is cool
took bedfellows for moons mountains for friends

—open your thighs to fate and(if you can
withholding nothing)World,conceive a man

# New Poems

POEMS 294 TO 315

# 294

---

un
der fog
's
touch

slo

ings
fin
gering
s

wli

whichs
turn
in
to whos

est

people
be
come
un

kind)
YM&WC
(of sort of)
A soursweet bedtime

-less un-
(wonderful)
story atrickling a
-rithmetic o-

ver me you & all those & that
"I may say professor"
asleep
wop "shapley

has compared the universe
to a
uh" pause
"Cookie

but" nonvisibly smi-
ling through man
-ufactured harmlessly accurate
gloom "I

think he might now be inclined to describe
it rather as
a" pause "uh"
cough

"Biscuit"
(& so on & so unto canned
swoonsong
came "I wish you good" the mechanical

dawn
"morning")& that those you
i St
ep

into the not
merely immeasurable into
the mightily alive the
dear beautiful eternal night

a football with white eyebrows the
3
rd chief something or must be off

duty wanderfuling aft spits)
int
o immensity(upon once whom

fiercely by pink mr seized green
mrs
opening is it horribly smith spouts

cornucopiously not unrecognizable whats of
t
oo vertiginously absorbed which à la

(of Ever-Ever Land i speak
sweet morons gather roun'
who does not dare to stand or sit
may take it lying down)

down with the human soul
and anything else uncanned
for everyone carries canopeners
in Ever-Ever Land

(for Ever-Ever Land is a place
that's as simple as simple can be
and was built that way on purpose
by simple people like we)

down with hell and heaven
and all the religious fuss
infinity pleased our parents
one inch looks good to us

(and Ever-Ever Land is a place
that's measured and safe and known
where it's lucky to be unlucky
and the hitler lies down with the cohn)

down above all with love
and everything perverse
or which makes some feel more better
when all ought to feel less worse

(but only sameness is normal
in Ever-Ever Land
for a bad cigar is a woman
but a gland is only a gland)

# 298

lucky means finding
Holes where
pockets aren't lucky
's to spend

laughter
not money lucky are
Breathe
grow dream

die love not
Fear eat sleep kill
and have you am luck
-y is we lucky luck-

ier
luck
-I-
est

# 299

Q:dwo
   we know of anything which can
   be as dull as one englishman
A:to

# 300

&-moon-He-be-hind-a-mills

tosses like thin bums dream
ing i'm thick in a hot young queen with

a twot with a twitch like kingdom
come(moon
The

sq
uirmwri
th-ing out of wonderful
thunder!of?ocean.a

ndn
ooneandfor
e-ver)moon She over this new eng
land fragrance of pasture and now ti

p toe ingt o
a child who alone st
and

s(not a
fraid of moon You)

not-mere-ly-won-der-ing-&

# 301

this little bride & groom are
standing)in a kind
of crown he dressed
in black candy she

veiled with candy white
carrying a bouquet of
pretend flowers this
candy crown with this candy

little bride & little
groom in it kind of stands on
a thin ring which stands on a much
less thin very much more

big & kinder of ring & which
kinder of stands on a
much more than very much
biggest & thickest & kindest

of ring & all one two three rings
are cake & everything is protected by
cellophane against anything(because
nothing really exists

so little he is
so.
     Little
ness be

(ing)
comes ex
-pert-
Ly expand:grO

w
  i
?n
   g

Is poet iS
(childlost
so;ul
)foundclown a

-live a
,bird
    !O
& j &

ji
&
jim,jimm
;jimmy

s:
  A
V
o(

  .

  :

  ;

 ,

# 303

nor woman
      (just as it be

        gan to snow he dis
        a

          ppeare
          d leavi
            ng on its

              elf pro
                pped uprigh
                t that in this o
              ther w

              ise how e
            mpty park bundl
           e of what man can

          't hurt any more h
        u

          sh
nor child)

my specialty is living said
a man(who could not earn his bread
because he would not sell his head)

squads right impatiently replied
two billion pubic lice inside
one pair of trousers(which had died)

# 305

The Mind's(

i never you never
he she or it

never we you and they never
saw so
much heard so much smelled so much

tasted
plus touched quite so And
How much nonexistence
eye sed bea

yew tea mis
eyesucks unyewkuntel finglestein idstings
yewrety oride lesgo eckshun

kemeruh daretoi
nig

)Ah,Soul

# 306

if i

or anybody don't
know where it her his

my next meal's coming from
i say to hell with that
that doesn't matter(and if

he she it or everybody gets a
bellyful without
lifting my finger i say to hell
with that i

say that doesn't matter)but
if somebody
or you are beautiful or
deep or generous what
i say is

whistle that
sing that yell that spell
that out big(bigger than cosmic
rays war earthquakes famine or the ex

prince of whoses diving into
a whatses to rescue miss nobody's
probably handbag)because i say that's not

swell(get me)babe not(understand me)lousy
kid that's something else my sweet(i feel that's

true)

# 307

hanged

if n
y in a real hot spell
with o

man

what bubbies going
places on such
babies aint plenty
good enough for

i

eu
can have
you

rope

# 308

economic secu
rity" is a cu
rious excu

se
(in

use among pu
rposive pu
nks)for pu

tting the arse
before the torse

# 309

beware beware beware
because because because
equals(transparent or

science must
bait laws with
stars to catch telescopes

)why.
Being is
patience is patient is(patiently

all the eyes of these with listening
hands only fishermen are
prevented by cathedrals

only as what(out of a flophouse)floats
on murdered feet into immense no

Where
        which to map while these not eyes quite try
almost their mind immeasurably roots
among much soundless rubbish of guitars
and watches
                only as this(which might have been
a man and kept a date and played a tune)
death's dollhead wandering under weakening stars

Feels;if
        & god said & there was
                                is born:
one face who.
                and hands hold his whose unlife
bursts


        only so;only if you should turn
the infinite corner of love,all that i am
easily disappears(leaving no proof

not the least shadow of a.  Not one smallest dream)

must being shall

one only thing must:the opening of a
(not some not every but any)
heart—wholly,idiotically—before
such nonsense which
is the overlove & underwish of
beauty;before keen if
dim quiveringly
spangle & thingless
& before flashing soft neverwheres &
sweet nothingly gushing tinsel;silently
yes before angel curvings upon a mostless
more of star

o-

pening of(writhing your exploding my)heart
before how worlds delicate
of bombast—papery what
& vast solidities,unwinding
dizzily &
mirrors;sprung dimensionless
new alls of joy:quietly & before illimitably
spiralling candy of tiniest
forever—crazily from totally sprouted by alive
green each very lifting
& seriously voice
-like finger of

the tree

# 312

may my heart always be open to little
birds who are the secrets of living
whatever they sing is better than to know
and if men should not hear them men are old

may my mind stroll about hungry
and fearless and thirsty and supple
and even if it's sunday may i be wrong
for whenever men are right they are not young

and may myself do nothing usefully
and love yourself so more than truly
there's never been quite such a fool who could fail
pulling all the sky over him with one smile

# 313

the people who
rain(are move as)proces
-sion Its oflike immens-
ely(a feet which is prayer

among)float withins he
upclimbest And(sky she
)open new(
dark we all findingly Spring the

Fragrance unvisible)ges
-tured together-
ly singing ams
trample(they flyingly silence

# 314

porky & porkie
sit into a moon)

blacker than dreams
are round like a spoon are
both making silence

two-made-of-one

& nothing tells anywhere
"snow will come soon" &
pretending they're birds sit

creatures of quills
(asleep who must go

things-without-wings

you shall above all things be glad and young.
For if you're young,whatever life you wear

it will become you;and if you are glad
whatever's living will yourself become.
Girlboys may nothing more than boygirls need:
i can entirely her only love

whose any mystery makes every man's
flesh put space on;and his mind take off time

that you should ever think,may god forbid
and(in his mercy)your true lover spare:
for that way knowledge lies,the foetal grave
called progress,and negation's dead undoom.

I'd rather learn from one bird how to sing
than teach ten thousand stars how not to dance